STAYING POWER

30 SECRETS INVINCIBLE EXECUTIVES USE FOR GETTING TO THE TOP —AND STAYING THERE

THOMAS A. SCHWEICH

Contemporary Books

Chicago   New York   San Francisco   Lisbon   London   Madrid   Mexico City
Milan   New Delhi   San Juan   Seoul   Singapore   Sydney   Toronto

The *McGraw·Hill* Companies

Library of Congress Cataloging-in-Publication Data

Schweich, Thomas A., 1960–
    Staying power : 30 secrets invincible executives use for getting to the top—and staying there / Thomas A. Schweich.
        p.   cm.
    Includes index.
    ISBN 0-07-139517-2
    1. Executive ability.   2. Leadership.   3. Management.   I. Title.

HD38.25.U6S39   2003
658.4'09—dc21   2003041986

2 3 4 5 6 7 8 9 0   AGM/AGM   2 1 0 9 8 7 6 5 4

ISBN 0-07-139517-2

McGraw-Hill books are available at special quantity discounts to use as premiums and sales promotions, or for use in corporate training programs. For more information, please write to the Director of Special Sales, Professional Publishing, McGraw-Hill, Two Penn Plaza, New York, NY 10121-2298. Or contact your local bookstore.

This book is printed on acid-free paper.

To my wife, Kathy, and my children,
Emilie and Thomas Jr.

Contents

Acknowledgments

I would like to thank my editor, Judith McCarthy, for her skill, encouragement, and enthusiasm. She is a true professional, and I have very much enjoyed working with her on my past two book projects. My agent, Wendy Sherman, has become one of my most trusted advisers, not only in my writing, but in life generally. My wife and family have been wonderful supporters—letting me toil away in my home office without interruption and with genuine support and excitement.

I would also like to thank the dozens of people who took time out to help me with the material for this book. It is my first book that required a lot of outside assistance. Thanks to my partners and associates at Bryan Cave who helped me line up interviews, including Chairman Walter L. Metcalfe Jr., Senator John C. Danforth, and Edward L. Dowd Jr. Thanks to my assistants Colleen Kashif and Alesia Carter for arranging the complex logistics of the interviews, typing up interview reports, and assisting me with the final edits to the book.

And thanks especially to the top leaders who took time out from their busy schedules to talk to me about their views on success. They are

Douglas G. Bain	Richard R. Bell
Andrew N. "Drew" Baur	Norma B. Clayton

Adam Clymer
Sheryl Crow
John C. "Jack" Danforth
Robert J. "Bob" Dole
Edward L. "Ed" Dowd Jr.
Patrick J. "Pat" Finneran
Samuel "Sam" Fox
Ronald J. Gafford
Richard A. Gephardt
Joel Gotler
Earl G. Graves
Thomas M. "Tom" Gunn
Juanita H. Hinshaw
Dr. Joshua Korzenik
Stephen K. Lambright
Christopher Lloyd
J. W. "Bill" Marriott Jr.

Thomas J. "Tom" O'Neill
James F. "Jim" Parker
Admiral Joseph Prueher
Janet Reno
Dave G. Ruf Jr.
Joseph Ryan
Lt. Gen. John B. Sams Jr.
Jack Schmitt
Bruno Schmitter
Michael M. "Mike" Sears
William "Bill" Shaw
Gina Shock
Alan K. Simpson
Barrett A. Toan
Hendrik A. Verfaillie
William "Bill" Winter

Introduction

"Most Unlikely to Succeed"

You may be the invincible executive, and you may not even know it. Big-time success is a complex and deceptive goal. Millions of people have the qualities necessary to become leaders in their fields, but they have not discovered their personal paths to the top. So they settle for mediocre careers that simply pay the bills. It does not have to be that way.

At the other extreme, many executives think that their careers are secure and on the rise when, actually, they are teetering on the edge of professional disaster. These people often suffer setbacks from which they never recover. Just look at the recent accounting and self-dealing scandals that have toppled senior executives of Tyco International, Global Crossing, Enron, Arthur Andersen, Xerox, Adelphia, and ImClone, to name a few. These executives thought they had it all, and then lost it in a flash. Such failures are avoidable.

This book organizes and analyzes the wisdom of a group of very successful people for the purpose of solving the mystery of professional victory. It will allow you to harness your best qualities and suppress those that make you vulnerable to failure. It will provide you the secrets of professional staying power, straight from the experiences of some of our country's most invincible executives.

The basic rules are the same no matter what your chosen field is—corporate executive, military officer, politician, entertainer, writer—you name it. We should start, however, with three threshold requirements to professional invincibility. First, you have to be smart. Not necessarily book-smart, but smart nonetheless. I assume that you are. If you're not, save your money and put the book back on the shelf. *All invincible executives are very smart.*

Second, you have to put your career at or very near the top of your priorities list. As we will discuss in detail shortly, invincible executives are engaged in an endless battle to balance their family and leisure interests with a job that *almost consumes them*. I assume you are waging that battle as well. If not, you will never be assured a place at the top.

Finally, you have to be honest. That does not mean you have to be a moralistic do-gooder. You can be tough, even ruthless, in certain circumstances; and you can take risks. But you have to know where "the line" is, and you can never cross it. We will cover some of those "lines" a little later.

Then, assuming you have the intellect, commitment, and integrity necessary to become invincible, you have to learn and execute thirty very basic tactics, continuously, for your entire professional life. Mark my words. All the brains, ambition, and good intentions in the world won't get you there unless you follow these rules. That's where I come in.

I decided to write a book about professional staying power one night when I was sitting in one of those black row-chairs next to Gate D3 at LaGuardia Airport in New York. The plane was an hour late, and I had arrived two hours early—only to find that there was no line at security. I found a sufferable position in the chair and then turned my attention to stretching *USA Today* into a three-hour read.

Within two minutes, I was interrupted—loudly—by a middle-aged man in a suit. "Hey you! Sir!"

"Yeah?" I asked, bothered, as if the man talking had diverted my eyes from the closing pages of *A Tale of Two Cities.*

He pointed to my luggage tag that had my business card on it. "You work at a big law office, right? One with like hundreds of lawyers all over the world?"

"Yes, I do."

"I had a friend in high school who went to work at your place after he spent some time at another law office. I was amazed he could even get a job with you guys. Jeez, in high school, he was a goof-off, you know, not exactly big-time law material. Yeah, I have thought about Walter many times, but I suspect he probably didn't last long at your place. You've probably never even heard of him."

"Walter who?" I asked, with a bit more interest.

"Walter Metcalfe."

I smiled. "Actually," I said, "he is the chairman of the firm."

The man was aghast. "No way! Walter? That's impossible."

"It's true."

He shook his head. "I cannot believe it!"

While this incident may have reflected some lingering high school jealousy, it got me thinking. That "goof-off" to whom the man referred had gone on to become the chairman of one of the most prestigious law firms in the country. He was listed by *The National Law Journal* as one of the one hundred most powerful attorneys in the United States. He hobnobbed with leading politicians, philanthropists, CEOs—even Alan Greenspan. How did he do that?

A couple of weeks later, I was having lunch with clients, and I listened to a conversation similar in tone about a woman named Susan. She was the senior vice president of human resources and administration at a multibillion-dollar financial institution. "She had *not even gone to business school,*" the better-educated (but less successful) lunch crowd lamented. A bank hired her out of college as an executive assistant—a glorified secretary, for heaven's sake!

Then came four mergers in eight years. After each merger, Susan got a promotion while she watched her peers get downsized and outsourced, or just barely hold on to what they had. Now Susan has 450 people reporting to her; she makes over $400,000 per year; and she has her former coworkers totally baffled by her unbridled success.

I know Walter and Susan—and many others like them—as the invincible executive. They have gotten where others aspire to be, and managed to stay there in tough times, and no one can quite figure out how. In the vast majority of cases, they are not the "Most Likely to Succeed" kids who then glide with ease—and seeming destiny—to professional success. Think about it. What happened to your Most Likely to Succeed classmate from high school? I do not even know where my Most Likely to Succeed is. It sure wasn't me.

More often than not, the invincible executive is a woman or man whose career seems guided less by the graceful hand of destiny than by something closer to a cattle prod—jolting her or him through glory and worry to the top of the corporate heap. My research reveals that the invincible executive does not get to the top easily and only rarely does so with grace. To borrow a somewhat overextended metaphor from a young CEO of a sporting goods franchise: the invincible executive "rides the wave of successful ventures aggressively like a surfer on the brink, but just as often he must emerge unscathed from the crashing waves of failure around him." Issues of prose aside, the man captures an important point. Others with good educations, intellect, and ambition fall into the vast ocean of corporate mediocrity. Yet the invincible executive advances, thrives, survives. He or she has staying power.

The head-shaking and bewilderment that invincible executives leave in their wakes suggest to me that their coworkers have a lot of trouble pinpointing those qualities that lead to meteoric careers. So I decided to get to the bottom of the issue of who gets to the top by profiling some seventy top executives—many of them seemingly invincible—whom I have encountered in my own career as a writer, lecturer, attorney, and prosecutor.

To get a uniquely comprehensive perspective, I went for a great deal of diversity in the type of people I profiled—not only in terms of gender, religion, political affiliation, and race, but also in the type of work they do. In fact, the people I discuss in this book have only one thing in common: they rose to the top of very competitive fields and stayed there for a long time. These fields included big business, finance, the military, politics, entertainment, writing, medicine, and law.

I conducted one-on-one interviews with forty of the seventy people I profiled. Some of the interviewees have become so successful that they are household names. However, I thought it was important that I also interview people with more modest success stories—such as owners of successful small and medium-sized businesses and people with humble backgrounds who became successful engineers or senior managers in large corporations. The higher-profile interviewees included people as wide-ranging as corporate legend Bill Marriott of Marriott International; Jim Parker, CEO of the United States' only profitable major airline, Southwest Airlines; upstart software CEO Barrett Toan of Express Scripts; former House Minority Leader Richard Gephardt; former Senator Bob Dole; ex–Attorney General Janet Reno; retired U.S. Navy Admiral and U.S. Ambassador to China Joseph Prueher; African-American entrepreneur extraordinaire Earl Graves; six-time Emmy-winning television producer Christopher Lloyd; and eight-time Grammy winner Sheryl Crow. The interviews often lasted two hours or more. Certain companies, like Marriott and Boeing, gave me access to a cross section of their top executives, which helped me glean corporate viewpoints that supplemented the thoughts and opinions of individual professionals with whom I spoke.

In other cases, I learned the views of senior professionals not through formal interviews, but by working with them on legal matters, business transactions, or civic events. For example, when I served as the chief of staff for Senator John Danforth's Waco investigation, I had the chance to interview, interface, and/or work with top professionals such as Senator Arlen Specter; General Pete Schoomaker (then commander in chief of the U.S. Special Operations Command); then Defense Secretary William Cohen; several top officials of the Justice Department, the Department of Defense, and the FBI; a couple of federal judges; and even ex-President Clinton. Through these and other experiences as a lawyer, speaker, and prosecutor, I made notes—often contemporaneously—of the behavior and insights of top executives as they performed their jobs. Many of these insights are included in this book as well—supplemented with research that I did on their careers.

Interestingly, people with careers ranging from "rock stars" to "four stars" say and do a lot of the same things—in somewhat different, but equally insightful, ways. When a top woman punk drummer with purple hair and a nose ring makes the same observation as a silver-haired man dripping with battle medals, we must have distilled some sort of truth about professional accomplishment. By conducting a wide-ranging survey of successful people, supplemented with my own professional research, I think I have finally figured out what makes the invincible executive.

This book is not deep. But the thirty rules that follow are powerful, and you can use them every day. While I acknowledge that invincible executives are multifaceted, profound, and, in many cases, difficult to pigeonhole, they are also very tactical people. Yes, they all have their complex inner selves, but they also cultivate their professional progress and personal images with nuts-and-bolts principles of conduct. I'll leave the profound observations on leadership and "team building" to others. We are going to cover the specific tactics that separate the most successful people from the crowd. This is not a book about professional psychology; it is a book about professional triumph.

In that practical spirit, I have concluded that invincible executives tend to follow thirty basic Rules of Invincibility, or ROIs for short. (Fittingly, the acronym, ROI, means "king" in French.) Once you strip away the intangibles, the ROIs of the invincible executive are simple and easily distilled. In many cases, they are absolutely Machiavellian—contrived and nearly calculating. In fact, one of the people I interviewed said that the title of the book ought to be *The New Prince: Machiavelli Visits the Twenty-First Century*. I took it as a compliment. Using the rules that I describe requires no apology—by the executives who use them, by me, or by you. They are the means—completely legitimate and ethical—by which talented people get to the top and stay there. Nothing wrong with that.

Few invincible executives adhere to every ROI, but a large majority adhere to most of them. The thirty ROIs relate to three principal areas: career path, personality characteristics, and management style. So I have divided this book into three parts: "The Invincible Career Path," "The Invincible Personality," and "The Invincible Management Style." There are ten rules on the career planning that leads to the invincible career path, ten rules on the inner characteristics that create the invincible professional personality, and ten management tenets that lead to an invincible style of organizing and harnessing the capabilities of other people.

Each of the thirty short sections has the same structure. First, I state the ROI. Then I provide the Snapshot results of a survey question I asked top professionals that ultimately led to the ROI. Following the survey question and answer, I elaborate on the ROI by giving you some of the specific thoughts of top executives with whom I discussed the issue. The process is simple, and the results might surprise you.

THE INVINCIBLE CAREER PATH

The first step to becoming a professional with staying power is to understand how top executives plan their careers. I studied their answers to questions like, How early did you know what you wanted to be in life? How focused were you on particular career goals? How big a role did luck play in your success? How did you know when to make your move? How have you handled failures or setbacks? Here are the fascinating answers that invincible executives gave to these and other questions about their career paths.

RULE

1

Do Not Map Out Your Career

SNAPSHOT

When you were starting your career, did you have a "career plan"?

Yes: 5 percent   **No:** 95 percent

In 1982, I met a supremely confident, arrogant, and highly intelligent young student at Harvard Law School. His name was Gary. One day at dinner, Gary lectured me on the keys to professional success. He said that the way to guarantee a great career was early planning and unbridled focus on specific goals. He then proceeded to announce that he would be on the prestigious *Harvard Law Review* by the end of the school year. He said that within twelve years, he would become a Republican senator from his home state of Kansas, just like his idol Senator Bob Dole. Gary said that within twenty-five years, he would "make a run" for the presidency. "You have got to know what you want and then go get it, Tom," he said, using words echoed by so many present-day gurus. He spoke with convincing conviction.

And sure enough, a few years later, Gary did "make a run." A run for the border. He had just jumped bail on federal drug and

3

gun trafficking charges. It seems that when his law practice did not immediately get him the wealth and glory that he sought, he turned to smuggling cocaine from Colombia. Eventually, the authorities apprehended him and he spent several years in prison. The man who had planned to be the symbol of our Stars and Stripes settled for the stripes. His sense of personal conviction resulted in a criminal conviction. What happened there?

The Problem of Focus

Gary was too focused. *Invincible executives are not.* During my many interviews of dozens of extremely successful people, one point that immediately hit me between the eyes is that invincible executives, while highly ambitious, rarely had specific, long-term career plans. Even more interesting, most believe that an intense focus on specific career goals is counterproductive to success.

I had a fascinating discussion on this issue with Gary's idol, Senator Bob Dole—a man who has lived most of Gary's dream. Senator Dole started out as anything but invincible. He suffered a permanent disability in World War II. He fought back from his health problems, and by the 1950s he had become a prominent local Kansas politician. After the senior U.S. senator from Kansas retired, Dole ran for U.S. Senate and won. Eventually, he became the Senate majority leader. Then he had a couple of setbacks. He ran for president in 1996 as the Republican nominee and lost. He also fought and beat prostate cancer. However, despite these setbacks, Senator Dole immediately resurrected his career as a major charitable fund-raiser, bestselling author, good-humored spokesperson for a series of high-profile products, and the effervescent husband of his high-flying political wife, Elizabeth. Senator Dole is a person who, despite serious health problems and political setbacks, has always seemed to emerge on top. At seventy-nine, he remains as well known and as popular as ever. This soldier has not faded away.

Like so many other successful people with whom I discussed the issue, Senator Dole told me right up front that he never had a career plan. After World War II, he was something of a local hero in Russell, Kansas, and that inspired him to try to make something of his life. Yes, he had ambition. But there was never a map; he never sat down and said, "This is what I want to be." He did not think much about becoming a U.S. senator when he was a state senator. And he did not think much about the presidency until President Ford picked him as his running mate in 1976.

"I think it was almost an accident that I got into politics," says Senator Dole. And once he got into it, he did not have a "step-by-step process" to get him to the top. Senator Dole believes that saying "I am going to be this or that" is just not the way success works. Success is simply not a "mappable quality." His words were echoed by former Wyoming Senator Alan Simpson, who told me that, when he was a young state legislator in Wyoming, he recalls a group of aspiring politicians who all said they would be governors or U.S. senators some day. Simpson, however, never said anything of the sort. As for those who did make these statements, "none of them made it," Simpson said. "They disappeared." Anyone with the arrogance to tell others what he or she will be in a decade is setting himself or herself up for a fall, according to Senator Simpson.

Artificial Goals

"People who set artificial career goals make a huge mistake," according to Jim Parker, CEO of Southwest Airlines. Parker, who started his career as a lawyer, recalls a meeting he had with Southwest Chairman Herb Kelleher many years ago. Parker was a young assistant attorney general for the state of Texas. Kelleher asked him what his career goals were. Parker replied, awkwardly, "Honestly, I never really have set any career goals." Kelleher looked back at him and smiled. "Then we are going to get along just fine," he said.

Both Parker and Kelleher believe that rigid professional planning is a major obstacle to long-term professional success. Indeed, the major mistake that causes otherwise talented people to fail, according to Parker, is "the desire to achieve some specific title or position at some specific time in your career."

The viewpoint expressed by Senator Dole and Mr. Parker is a recurring theme among the invincible executives we shall get to know in this book. Let's start with recording artists. Grammy winner Sheryl Crow told me that in 1986, she just picked up and left her teaching job in St. Louis and headed for Los Angeles with four thousand dollars in her pocket. Within a few years, she was the most decorated rock star in the world. "I didn't have any plan for how I would get a record deal," she said. "I just figured the first thing I would do was . . . try to see what I could do as far as getting my music heard. . . . My plan wasn't even remotely reality-based," Crow added. Rock drummer Gina Shock told me virtually the same story. In 1979, she loaded up her drums in her car and drove to Los Angeles. She had no idea that she and her band, the Go-Go's, would hit number one less than three years later, and she had no specific plan on how to get there.

How different can rock stars and military leaders be? Well, in terms of career planning, they are not that different at all. Admiral Joseph Prueher said that he never thought that he would become the commander of the Pacific Fleet when he started his career as a young officer. His only goal was to serve his country the best way that he could. "Planning is an eight-lane highway," according to Admiral Prueher. "You really have to keep a lot of options open," he adds. "Another way to look at it is to consider yourself to be at the center of a circle, with the option of going in any direction. If your plan is 360 degrees, you don't have a plan. If it is 180 degrees, it is probably not a functional plan. If you can get it down to a quadrant—90 degrees—then you are doing pretty well." No one should be more focused than that.

Pat Finneran, the former marine who is in charge of some of the nation's largest military programs for Boeing, also could "never have dreamed" he would be responsible for thousands of people and billions of dollars when he joined the marines as a lieutenant in 1966. "I did not have specific plans. . . . I felt a need to support my country in the Vietnam conflict . . . so going into the Marine Corps just made sense to me at that time." His marine career gave him the qualifications to land a mid-level job at Boeing, and before he knew it, he had been promoted four times and had several thousand people reporting to him.

Perhaps the best examples of leading professionals who started with little in the way of plans are women lawyers over the age of fifty. When they went to law school from 1950 into the early 1970s, opportunities for women lawyers were very limited—big law firms would not hire them, and judges were usually white males. For that reason, they really could not have much in the way of specific plans. For example, former Attorney General Janet Reno told me that when she graduated from law school, her only ambition was to find a job—any job—in the legal profession. It never crossed her mind that she would become the chief law enforcement officer of even the local county when she was struggling to get a legal job in the 1960s. "Women were just not given opportunities in law back then," and her only ambition was to make a statement that women could succeed in a male-dominated field.

Similarly, Supreme Court Associate Justice Sandra Day O'Connor, who visited my law firm a few years back, told a story about how, after graduating from Stanford Law School, she tried to get a job as an associate attorney at a leading law firm. The law firm managers told her that they did not hire women, but they offered her a secretarial job. Decades later, after President Reagan had appointed Justice O'Connor to the Supreme Court, the same firm that had offered her a secretarial job when she was starting out invited her to speak to its lawyers. Justice O'Connor accepted the invitation and then took some pleasure in telling the members of the firm about the job that they had offered her so many years ago.

All of these top professionals had two things in common: the drive to succeed in their chosen fields and no specific plans on how to do so.

Four Reasons Not to Plan Your Career

There are several reasons why the invincible executive generally does not develop a specific career plan. The reasons range from the practical to the near-philosophical. First, if you are always looking ahead, you do not know where you are. You will not perform well in your current job. According to Mike Sears, the executive vice president and CFO of Boeing, "Life comes in bits and pieces. You get your teeth into a job that you like, and you enjoy it, and you work it. . . . Most of us have not, early on, set some very lofty position type goals. Rather, we have taken what we have and demonstrated good performance." It is always better, according to Sears, to focus on your current job and do it very well, while keeping your eyes open for the next opportunity.

Six-time Emmy-winning producer Christopher Lloyd (who has written for or produced "Frasier," "Wings," and "Golden Girls") told me that virtually the same rules apply in Hollywood. "You just sort of put your head down and do the best job you can at the level that you are at. There are always going to be people who are looking to advance you because, by advancing you, it makes their job easier. However, do not try to advance too fast. It is always great to take a step up the ladder, but do not do it unless you are really sure that you never want to be on the rung that you just left behind. Better to take it one rung at a time, because if you take two at a time, it is easier to [get in over your head and] fall back down. If you are on a slow rise to the top, I think you are sort of protecting yourself and not leaving yourself open to disappointment."

Hendrik Verfaillie, former CEO of the agricultural products company Monsanto, echoed these sentiments when he noted that one of the most important characteristics of top executives is that they channel their energies into doing a stellar job *right now.* Congressman Richard Gephardt agrees. He notes that the biggest mistake young people make early in their careers is an "unwillingness to start at the bottom." Congressman Gephardt believes that the best route to the top is to start somewhere at the bottom, learn about your profession in an unhurried manner, do a good job at whatever level you find yourself, and keep your eyes open for opportunity.

Second, it was a recurring theme in my interviews that, if you are going to succeed, people have to like you, and you have to like yourself. If you spend your time telling everyone where you should be or where you intend to be in your career, your pride and arrogance will turn people against you. Pushing for a particular job or title, according to Jim Parker of Southwest Airlines, "destroys the cooperation of your peers." Consequently, it is the quickest way to make professional enemies. In fact, the sentiment that you should be in a better place than you are is, according to over fifteen of the people I interviewed, the single biggest reason why people fail to realize their potential. While inner ambition must be very strong, its external manifestation must on a day-to-day basis be very mild. Most invincible executives agree that there are only a couple of times in most successful careers when you have to make an aggressive move. We'll cover those rare occasions shortly, but the general rule is to work hard and lie low.

In addition, according to Stephen Lambright, a group vice president of Anheuser-Busch, if your eyes are always a rung or two above your current place on the professional ladder, you will be continually frustrated with your progress. This frustration can and often does lead people into self-destructive professional behavior, such as bad-mouthing others who are promoted ahead of them or demanding concessions from employers when the employees are in a position of weakness. "Their ambitions become their own worst enemy in that they don't move fast enough on their own schedule and they either give up or burn out," according to Lambright. Many career flameouts can be attributed directly to the pride, arrogance, self-pity, and even self-loathing that arise from a rigidly charted career path that isn't going exactly according to plan.

Keeping your ambition in soft focus is, therefore, essential to maximizing professional opportunity. Indeed, several of the invincible executives I interviewed said that if you are too focused on a specific goal, you foreclose opportunities for success in areas outside of your narrow focus. "You never know exactly where that opportunity might arise," Hollywood superagent Joel Gotler told me. In fact, most invincible executives have made major changes in their career paths. For example, Condoleezza Rice, the national security advisor, thought at one time that her path to glory would be as a classically trained professional musician. Had she limited her opportunities to music, we would have never had the benefits of her diplomatic and political skills.

Finally, at the highest plane, invincible executives are quick to point out that neither science nor human nature favor focused career planning. The late medical researchers William Masters and Virginia Johnson put it to me roughly this way when I had the chance to talk to them at length several years ago in connection with a civic event. Since individual personalities are fluid and the events that surround us are equally fluid, any attempt to be overly rigid in living one part of life will result in a sort of counterreaction—the emergence of disorder in other areas of life. The future does not like being constrained and reacts against it.

Put more specifically in the career context, Doug Bain, senior vice president and general counsel of Boeing, notes, "You cannot plot your career from here to there because the facts and the world around you will change." Overplanning runs contrary to the way the universe works—according to everyone from medical researchers to corporate vice presidents.

"Look at our presidents," a former senior staffer at the Smithsonian Institution noted to me in an off-the-record, social context a few months ago. "Leaders who sort of meandered their way to the presidency, like Ronald Reagan, Abraham Lincoln, and George W. Bush, seem to lack the tragic flaws of those who focused and planned for their presidencies at an early age like Richard Nixon and Bill Clinton did." True, he added, it is possible to get to your goal with unbridled focus—both Nixon and Clinton did—but (1) it is very hard to do, with most people failing miserably, and (2) those very few who do succeed with unrelenting focus are often emotionally stunted, which can in turn lead to corruption, scandal, and a tragic fall. That was certainly the case with President Nixon, and arguably so with President Clinton. It is no surprise that the two presidents who were most focused on reaching the presidency experienced the most turmoil when they got there—the former resigning and the latter getting impeached. Indeed, "the more focused the action, the stronger the counterreaction," to paraphrase Sir Isaac Newton.

The tendency of focus and overly rigid planning to backfire is a common thread in my research. A highly intelligent and respected deacon with whom I spoke recently blamed the scandals in the Roman Catholic Church on a similar phenomenon—a rigid priestly lifestyle designed to promote lofty goals often leads to a secret underworld of shameful conduct. "Rigid structures crack the most easily," he said. "When overly focused people fall, they fall big." Remember Gary from the beginning of this chapter? Same idea.

An actor's agent echoed essentially the same sentiment when he told me several years ago that he has seen many would-be stars focus so intently on becoming famous that, even if they are among the very few who reach their goals, they are by that time often broken, emotionally empty, and riddled with addictions and personality disorders. "Forcing your mind into obsessive focus on specific goals effectively mortgages other areas of your personal and professional development, leading to self-destructive conduct," he observed.

While I have no specific opinion on clergy celibacy or how to succeed in Hollywood, I was fascinated at the parallels between what I heard from prominent businesspeople, sociologists, historians, and religious leaders on the subject of rigid professional goals: it is not the best route to success and often leads to catastrophic failure.

So lesson number one for all would-be invincible executives is that ambition is good, but it is better to leave your ambition to work its way through life without rigidly focused goals and step-by-step planning. That is not to suggest that we should avoid goals entirely. But the invincible executive charts a general direction, not a specific result. His or her goals are impressionistic—colorful, fluid, multifaceted—but above all, imprecise.

Discover Your Talents Early, and Discard Your Fantasies Immediately

---

📷 SNAPSHOT

Do you believe in the oft-stated paradigm that "you can be anything you want to be if you just put your mind to it"?

Yes: 5 percent   **No:** 95 percent

Recently, I conducted an important study from my living room couch—with a couple of cold beers serving as my survey assistants. I counted the number of times someone being interviewed on TV said words to the effect that "you can be anything you want if you just put your mind to it." Equivalent statements included:

"Hold on to your dreams and you can achieve anything."

"Don't ever give up and eventually you will get where you want to go."

"All you need is perseverance. You *will* get there."

By the end of one week, watching an average of two hours a day of television, I heard statements of this kind from seven athletes, four actors/actresses, three talk-show hosts, two authors, two singers, and one business tycoon. I heard it nineteen times in one week of prime-time couch-potato television. As I was writing this chapter, I read a newspaper article in which several young entertainment stars—from rappers to television idols—promised kids that they could be anything that they wanted to be. "There is never an obstacle too big that you can't overcome if you put your mind and resources to it," according to rapper Big Tigger.

In my opinion, few—if any—of these people believe what they are saying. The media trainers tell them to say it: if an interviewer starts pandering to you, tell the audience that you are nothing special; tell them that they could just as easily be where you are. Statements of encouragement to fans and wanna-bes make the superstars seem modest, and they give those aspiring to success the opportunity to fantasize that they too could become dizzyingly famous in any field of their fantasy. But, based on my interviews, I do not believe that the people who spew out this baloney really think that you can be anything you want.

Singer Celine Dion made one of these "you can be anything" statements at a concert. But Celine has perfect pitch; they don't. Less than one in a million will get where she got in the recording world. And Kevin Garnet said in an interview words to the effect that all young basketball players can get to the NBA if they just work toward their dreams. Well sorry, Kevin, if you are 5'8" and can't jump, there is no way you are going to be a $100 million basketball star no matter how much time and energy you may devote to the cause.

More often than not, the reality is that hard work and a dream will not get you where you want to be. So what will?

Test Your Talents in Many Areas

We have already learned that rigid focus is not the path to professional success. The lesson here is: neither is the other extreme—

unrealistic dreaming. "Temper your optimism with realism about what you can achieve," says Admiral Prueher, whom we met previously. Indeed, the invincible executive is starkly realistic. When confronted with the issue head-on, almost all invincible executives acknowledge that *you cannot be anything you want to be.* In order to succeed you need two things: talent and luck. We'll cover luck in a later section. We'll cover talent in this one.

The invincible executive discards his or her fantasies, but also knows his or her talents. "There are so many things out there that you can be good at; your job is to find the areas where you excel," says William Lindsley, the owner of a top college career counseling and standardized testing preparation company. "So many new college graduates, as well as young and even mid-level executives, pick their careers haphazardly. They do not know themselves well enough to choose the right career field."

Invincible executives are adept at the process of "skill determination." They use their family background, education, and other life experiences to test their abilities in many areas—often, but not always, starting when they are very young. Most invincible executives have played instruments as children, taken a crack at writing plays or poetry, studied foreign languages, and/or tried multiple sports. As they test their skills, they rely heavily on mentors—teachers, relatives, and friends who have experienced a lot of life and who help them find the areas in which they truly excel. They use people of great experience and wisdom as foils against whom they bounce off their ideas for improving themselves, and they seek advice on possible professional directions.

Invincible executives also have a tendency to be well-traveled—either literally or figuratively. Adam Clymer, Washington correspondent for the *New York Times*, believes that seeing a lot of the United States, and, if possible, foreign countries, early in one's life or career is an important ingredient to long-term success. Indeed, many invincible executives with whom I spoke have had the good fortune to live in another country and see an entirely different cultural perspective on the world. Some had relatives in other countries and spent the summers living with them.

Ron Gafford, CEO of construction giant Austin Industries, has observed that many invincible executives are ex-military or were military brats. The military brats were exposed to a variety of cultures at an early age because their parents were stationed in different parts of the world, and that exposure gave them a broad-based perspective and good people skills. "They tend to be extroverts, more worldly, and good at making new friends" as a result of their travels, according to Gafford. And, as the daughter of a very successful diplomat once pointed out to me, "you have to see a lot of things that you *could be* good at in order to figure out what you *are* good at." Exposure to a broad base of culture gives people valuable perspective and an outgoing personality to go along with it.

Norma Clayton, a protégé of Jack Welch at General Electric who went on to become a senior executive at Boeing, is an African-American woman who grew up in a rural area of New Jersey. Life in her hometown was simple, mundane, and not without prejudice. "Your world could become very introverted," she noted. However, Ms. Clayton's mother worked for a French bank and frequently traveled to New York City. She made a point of taking Ms. Clayton with her to Wall Street on many occasions. "I was always excited about what she did—the big city, the machines. So I had an opportunity to really learn from her what it's like to be in business. . . . And when I began to go to New York City, in the business district, I saw all different types of people so that I knew the world was different from where I was growing up." The combination of seeing so many people of differing cultural backgrounds mixing together and admiring the awe-inspiring engineering feats around her inspired her to find her true talent. She became an engineer, thereby starting her path to the top.

In the case of those invincible executives who lacked the resources to travel, many of them immersed themselves in books about different countries and history. A couple of them told me that they developed fantasy worlds when they were children—pretending to be from China or France, or in one case, from ancient Rome! In fact, Norma Clayton said that she often fantasized about being "Madeline the French orphan roaming around Paris." It is a common thread among invincible executives that they get diverse perspectives on life and use those perspectives to find and develop their talents.

There can be no doubt that, if you have had broad cultural perspective early in life, you are more likely to learn your talents and enter a field where you will excel. If you have not had these experiences during youth, you will be more likely to take the path of least resistance, even if it means never discovering your true talents.

Find Your Area of Expertise

Remember, however, it is never too late to engage in the process of skill determination. I can tell you story after story of successful careers that started after forty. Frank McCourt started his career as a Pulitzer Prize–winning writer in his sixties by turning an avocation into a profession. Colonel Sanders was almost fifty when he realized his talent for producing tasty fast food on a massive scale. The earlier you start looking, however, the more likely it is that you will find your field of excellence while you still have enough time to make a name for yourself.

It is a sad fact that there are millions of people out there who are toiling in mediocrity because they never discovered their great skill in life. According to a top Beverly Hills agent, Joel Gotler, the more you see or read, the more you learn, and the more you learn about yourself, the more likely it is that you will find some thing or things at which you truly excel. Unfortunately, few people make the effort to find their areas of expertise.

Look at it this way. There are so many fields of opportunity that there are bound to be a couple of them where *you* rank among the best. If you want to become the invincible executive, therefore, you must test your skills in many areas as early in life as you possibly can. Do not let the fear of failure limit your experimentation. I wonder how many middle managers could be in the New York Philharmonic if they had just picked up a violin. More than you might expect.

Divide Your Interests into Three Categories: Fantasy, Avocation, and Talent

At some point, however, you need to start refining the skill determination process by moving in some general direction. By the time you are a few years into your career, if not earlier, you should be dividing your interests roughly into three categories: fantasies, avocations, and talents. Fantasies are those areas where you have determined that your skill level is too low for you to become a professional. Let go of any pretense that you will succeed in these areas. Do not waste your limited time and energy developing these skills other than as an occasional, compartmentalized outlet for your fantasies. As we said before, you cannot be anything you want to be.

For example, agent Joel Gotler told me that he wanted to be a novelist when he was younger. He read like a maniac. He wrote a lot, too. But soon he realized that he just was not going to make it as a writer. He could write pretty sentences but could not get the story told. So he abandoned his dream to become a writer and never looked back.

Avocations, on the other hand, are areas where you have enough talent that, under the right circumstances, you might be able to excel in that field. "You have to assess your talent . . . and [ask yourself] if this is going to be an avocation or a job," according to Norma Clayton. I know an engineer who is quite talented as a painter. He has painted attractive still life oils for friends and family, and he has submitted his work to shows with enough success to know that his dream of becoming a famous painter is not a complete fantasy. Someday he may make it big, so he should never give up on that avocation. In fact, while he has not yet gotten his work displayed at the Metropolitan Museum of Art, he has kept his eyes open for other opportunities to advance his artistic endeavors. To his great satisfaction, he has taught art to disabled children, writes art reviews as a paid critic for the local newspaper, and makes a lot of money appraising art for a trust company. In fact, he has established quite a reputation for himself in these endeavors—making frequent television and radio appearances in his city.

This man has a hip-pocket avocation that already brings him some success. Interestingly, most invincible executives do. I mentioned earlier that National Security Adviser Condoleezza Rice is an excellent pianist; a top lawyer friend of mine is a pretty good weekend racecar driver; another legal eagle friend is a regional triathlon champion; my mentor, Senator John Danforth, is an Episcopal priest. And, while not invincible but trying, I am a numismatic writer and coin collector.

Invincible executives always have interesting avocations (and I don't mean golf) because they have multidirectional minds that they have devoted to discovering their own talents. As a result, they have developed multiple areas of expertise. Anyone who really adopts the skill determination mind-set that all invincible executives have will almost by definition find two or three areas in which he or she has real potential.

In fact, sometimes you only have to make minor adjustments to your fantasies to turn them into professional success. As I mentioned earlier, Joel Gotler, who abandoned his dream of becoming a novelist, made it big representing novelists and screenwriters. Drew Baur, the chairman and CEO of Southwest Bank, was an athlete when he was in high school. But he quickly realized that he lacked the ability to become a professional ball player. Nevertheless, he recognized that his knowledge of baseball—combined with his banking skills—was an avocation that was still worth pursuing. So he spent as much time as he could learning the *business* of baseball. Eventually, he helped put together an ownership group that bought a major league team. He feels like he is living his fantasy, but none of it would have happened without a healthy dose of realism and the necessary adjustments that turned the fantasy of being a player into the reality of being an owner. I have never met a more professionally satisfied man.

Don't Confuse Academic Success with Professional Potential

Enough about avocations. True talents, on the other hand, are those areas where you know that you are among the best in the area in which you are competing. Many people confuse true talent with academic talent. Performance in specific academic areas—while relevant—does not tell the whole story. A top chef told me that he was so bad in almost every subject that his teachers and guidance counselors had him convinced he had no talents. They didn't teach cooking, and now he is the celebrity cooking guru in his large Western town.

Many people have resigned themselves to failure in life because they did not excel academically. Let me tell you something from personal experience. I went to Harvard Law School, and I wouldn't let at least half of the people I met there get anywhere near my legal work. As Stephen Lambright of Anheuser-Busch put it, "some people are very, very smart intellectually, but they cannot walk across the street without being hit by a car." There are so many skills that are not taught in our schools—the creativity and common sense that lead to invention; the momentum-building skills that make an effective manager; the perspective that molds a corporate leader; the ability to assess risk that causes a business owner to succeed. You may have all those skills bubbling under a C-minus average. Do not use your experiences in school as the sole or even principal measure of your potential. Yes, you have to be smart to be invincible. No, you do not have to have an A-plus average in school.

Apply Talents with the Broadest Brush Possible

When you have figured out what your talents are, develop them aggressively—but again, with soft focus—meaning that you apply the talent with as broad a brush as possible. So, for example, if you are an exceptional writer, don't focus all of your energy and effort on becoming an award-winning screenwriter. Writing movies is as tough a field as there can be, so try your hand at other facets of that same talent—books, news reporting, speechwriting, even Web design (which, contrary to appearances, does require writing skill if the site is to be successful). There are so many fields where top writing skills are needed. Keep all your options open and active.

By not focusing on specific goals, while simultaneously determining and developing your greatest talents, you have positioned yourself to take advantage of the real wild card of professional invincibility: *opportunity*. The next two sections, on flexibility and fortuity respectively, deal with the two facets of a critical skill— the capacity to recognize, maximize, and capitalize on opportunity. The soft focus and skills development that we have covered already lay the groundwork for maximizing these opportunities.

RULE

3

Maintain Pervasive Professional Flexibility

📷 **SNAPSHOT**

Is flexibility an essential element of professional success?

Yes: 96 percent   **No:** 4 percent

According to former Senator Alan Simpson, flexibility is essential to a successful career because unpredictability is the way of the universe. "These guys who wake up with their days all planned out on a Palm Pilot and a computer notebook, well God bless 'em," says Simpson. "I am here to say to them that I have never found a single day in my life that worked out the way that I planned it. Not a single day."

Stephen Hawking—among other leading popular physicists—writes book after book telling us how the universe, while seemingly rigid, is actually quite flexible. Space bends time; matter can be condensed and expanded. For many of us, it all seems interesting but very far away. Not for the invincible executive. The fact is we can apply those seemingly distant principles to improving our professional lives.

Most invincible executives have a very broad perspective on the world around them. They develop not only the cultural interests that we discussed earlier, but also historic and scientific interests. "We learn through anomalies," notes leading medical researcher Dr. Joshua Korzenik. The most successful people, according to Dr. Korzenik, are those who expose themselves to a wide variety of scientific and cultural ideas, and whose minds are always working to reconcile the anomalies that they see in those diverse concepts. This scientific sense of curiosity prevents "stasis"—the cessation of learning, says Korzenik. Indeed, most top professionals are intrigued by space, time, and matter and have learned to use these elements of the universe to their professional advantage. It seems they have all read Hawking's *A Brief History of Time.*

Invincible executives are, therefore, as flexible as the universe itself. Since the universe is composed of a flexible continuum of space, time, and matter, it should be no surprise that top professionals show a profound understanding and flexibility in terms of all three of these qualities. "Your goal is not to find the job that you need, but rather the one that needs you," according to aerospace executive Tom Gunn. And that process—locating your future—requires both a strong perspective on what is going on around you and a great deal of flexibility, according to Gunn. Let's talk about the specific areas where you need to be flexible so that you find the right path to success.

Geographic Fluidity

Let's start with "space." Most invincible executives agree that you cannot tie your career to a particular location in this world. Almost all of them have made significant geographic moves in their careers. They do not foreclose opportunities by limiting their careers to a particular city or even country. If the opportunity to advance means you have to pick up and move, then you must do so. In fact, over 80 percent of those invincible executive I interviewed have moved at least twice in their careers, with the average move being over 850 miles away from their previous homes.

You may decide that family stability or the love of a city means that you will *never move*. I know many people who have made that lifestyle choice, and they are very happy. It is an admirable choice and I commend them for it. But they will never be invincible executives. Geographic flexibility is a prerequisite to professional invincibility. As Doug Bain, the senior vice president and general counsel of Boeing, put it, you cannot limit your career path to a particular location or division of your company if you want to get to the top. "One of the biggest challenges I have is getting people to move geographically. Sometimes the opportunities are elsewhere," he notes, and by insisting that you stay in one place, you "may be losing out on those opportunities."

That is not to say you jump at any opportunity to move. If you work at a company that has 90 percent of its operations in your city, there should be a strong presumption that you will stay in that city because that is where the action is in terms of key people and decisions. However, if a move is likely to advance you professionally, you have to make that move even if there might be adverse social or family consequences.

Salvador's Clock

An upwardly mobile aerospace executive recently told me about the Salvador Dali museum in Paris—tucked away in a little basement near Montmartre. It is full of those paintings of barren landscapes and dripping watches that made Dali so famous. Dali is out of favor as an artist these days, but this guy insisted that I go to this museum even if it meant missing some better-known museums. "Why?" I asked. "Because Dali manipulated time better than anyone who ever lived."

The invincible executive understands the importance and flexibility of time and takes advantage of it. He or she is not a prioritizer, but rather a multitasker—capable of doing several things well at once and shifting focus effortlessly from one task to another. Former treasury secretary and Citigroup executive Robert Rubin often irritates coworkers who do not know him well because he will, for example, write a letter on one subject during a meeting on another subject. But he remains fully engaged in both topics. He does not view time as linear; he views it as malleable—capable of being molded to accommodate the tasks at hand, whatever they may be.

As we will discuss later, oftentimes an issue (or simple common courtesy to a boss or customer) will require your full attention, but even so, you must develop the capacity to do more than one thing at a time and then use that talent judiciously. The invincible executive does not watch the clock; he or she controls it and can actually seem to distort it in his or her favor. Some of the key areas where invincible executives manipulate time are routine. For example, many top executives set limits on the time a particular meeting will last. They know that they can drive issues to conclusions by telling people at the outset that a particular meeting has to end in forty-five minutes.

Many top executives also believe it is difficult to do top-quality work after a couple of years in the same job at a company. "The more assignments you have, the more opportunities you are going to have for learning. . . . I think that somewhere between eighteen and thirty months on a job and you are way up the learning curve," says Boeing's executive vice president and CFO Mike Sears. After that, according to Sears's colleague Norma Clayton, your job is reduced to "just making doughnuts." Indeed, anyone who has spent a lot of time observing numerous corporate environments as I have can tell you that after a couple of years in the same position, people start focusing on protecting their empires and the enterprise becomes secondary. Consequently, top professional leaders make it a policy to move people to different jobs after a certain period of time. They get results by controlling both time and space in this manner.

The Time-Momentum Equation

In other cases, the manipulation of time is less tangible. For example, one of the great skills that invincible executives have is the ability to build *momentum* in a project. Momentum is the acceleration of work within a set time period. It requires the ability to inspire, cajole, push, and drive a project toward a conclusion such that more gets accomplished in a shorter period of time than anyone could have possibly imagined at the outset of a project. The process can also be envisioned as the stretching of time "like a piece of chewing gum," as a patent-holding industrial engineer told me, to allow more to occur during a set interval.

Invincible executives build momentum by transferring their vision and enthusiasm for a particular project to their colleagues with both a carrot and a stick. The carrot is incentive—knowledge that success will bring specifically defined rewards. Invincible executives give their coworkers a "picture of the conclusion"—a vision of what the professional landscape will look like after the project is successfully accomplished, according to former Senator and Waco Special Counsel John Danforth. They allow others to visualize the greatness of the future. In effect, they manipulate time through the effective presentation today of a positive tomorrow. This process builds momentum and makes time work in favor of the group.

The stick is risk—knowledge that failure will have negative repercussions. Invincible executives tacitly paint the bleak picture of failure in the future—a subliminal parallel universe in which things are not going well. Remember, however, the carrot is in the foreground and is the focus of discussion; the stick is an undercurrent in the background. The invincible executive is always adept at manipulating time by building momentum in this fashion.

The invincible executive also knows when the flexibility of time must end. Leading medical researcher and academic Dr. Joshua Korzenik, for example, believes that flexibility in the area of medical research is critical. However, one of the biggest flaws among those who ultimately fail, he notes, is the inability to "realize that you are done." You should take as many detours as you need to take to ensure the integrity of your work, but eventually you have to arrive at a destination, according to Korzenik. Part of successful time manipulation involves ending a project cleanly.

Flex and Flack

A lot of people are not going to like this paragraph, but do not kill the messenger—I am reporting what I learned from the best. Harnessing time successfully often means that you have to get others to work to your schedule. Invincible executives usually resist what one of them termed "out of sync" work patterns. Most invincible executives, for example, do not favor "flextime" employees who do not work five days a week or employees who work different hours than everyone else in the organization. Some of them put up with it; few of them like it. They generally do not mind employees working off-site, but they find part-timers to be frustrating. For most invincible executives in traditional corporate environments, flextime puts the individual's schedule ahead of the enterprise schedule. It reduces the capacity of the executive to control time.

The legendary August Busch III of Anheuser-Busch fame, for example, has, I am told, made it clear to his direct reports that if he is at the office and needs some advice, and the person whose advice he needs is not available due to some sort of flexible schedule, he will hold the flex employee's *boss* responsible for any cost increase, schedule slippage, customer relations problems, or legal issues that arise because of the incompatible scheduling of his time with that of his employees. He does not prohibit employees whose schedules are out of sync with his, but he prevents it from interfering with the goals of the organization by adding a layer of responsibility for any negative repercussions.

As the world becomes increasingly technologically connected, the issue of out-of-sync timing will likely diminish. People will be able to use technology to make themselves accessible in an emergency at any time. This may not be good from a standpoint of quality of life, but it will, I predict, soften the view of most invincible executives that alternative work schedules hinder an employee's ability to progress. That means that if you have one of these flexible schedules, you should take extra steps to make yourself accessible by phone or e-mail. You should have specific discussions with your superiors about your accessibility—particularly how to reach you in the event of an emergency.

Start as a Specialist, but Become a Leader

However, flexibility in dealing with space and learning to twist time favorably are only two-thirds of the battle. The invincible executive is flexible in "matter" as well—matter being in this case the subject matter of his or her profession. Most invincible executives have switched professional disciplines completely at least one time. Bill Marriott changed the direction of his family's business from food services to hotels; Mike Sears of Boeing moved from engineering to program management to finance; Secretary of State Colin Powell and Admiral Joseph Prueher moved from war to politics and diplomacy—as have warriors from George Washington to Dwight Eisenhower before them.

To become invincible, you cannot be known as an engineer, accountant, or information systems guru. You must be known as a leader. That means you can start as a specialist, but you can never stay one. Specialists can do well in the world, but only generalists are invincible. According to the CEO of a midsized public relations company, "When you are starting out, people are looking for knowledge and skill with a little leadership mixed in. However, as you begin to achieve success, people are looking more for leadership with a little knowledge and skill mixed in. The higher you get, the more you can rely upon technical experts for the details. You are capable of an ever-increasing realm of leadership—often in fields for which you had no formal training." Or, as Doug Bain, the general counsel of Boeing, put it, "I keep telling people about the whole idea of flexibility. If all you want to do is work in this specialty, in this location, and in this division, you are really hurting your chances of getting ahead. If you want to focus just on being a high-level narrow specialist, you may be cutting your own throat. It's breadth of experience that you need to move ahead."

As invincible executives move seamlessly from one field to another, they must walk an increasingly wider path—i.e., increase the number of subject matters over which they can exercise confidence and control. Soon they become known simply for being good at whatever they do. Flexibility includes, therefore, stretching your professional length *and your professional width*. "Cut a wider and wider swath," a successful small business owner once told me. "As you go wider in your responsibilities, you will go higher in your organization."

Bill Marriott told me an interesting story along these lines. In 1956, the Marriott organization was a restaurant company. It had no hotels. Company officials decided to open a hotel, but they did not know who would run it. "We did not have anyone who could supervise the overall operation of the hotel," Marriott noted. "I asked if I could do it. And they looked at me like I was crazy. They said, 'You don't know anything about the hotel business.' And I said, 'I know, but neither does anybody else around here.' So I began supervising that first hotel, and then we opened a second, and then a third and fourth and I never looked back." Mr. Marriott surrounded himself with experts in the field and demonstrated his capacity to lead those people. Ultimately, his decision to widen the swath of his expertise led him to become the most famous hotel operator in history.

So here is what we have learned so far. Have ambition but don't have a plan. Determine and develop your skills as early as possible. Use those talents to achieve enough success that you are known as much for your success and leadership abilities as for your specific skills. Develop this reputation by adopting a flexible approach to space, time, and matter that will allow you to branch out to new and different areas such that your skill is *leadership* and the initial field of your skill becomes increasingly irrelevant. We're making progress.

RULE

4

Get Lucky

📷 **SNAPSHOT** ────────────────────────

What role does luck play in achieving great professional success?

Significant: 90 percent   **Insignificant:** 10 percent

A few months ago, I was talking to Gina Shock, the drummer (and, I understand, one of the best musicians) in the rock group the Go-Go's. The band had just made a successful comeback with a highly rated VH-1 special and new tour after many years of band members doing solo projects. Ms. Shock, admittedly nursing a hangover, told me about the early success of the band. "In 1979, I was just another girl with a dream of becoming a rock star. Like all the others, I packed my stuff up in my car and headed to L.A. Three years later, we were number one on the charts."

I asked her point blank: "What is it that you had that all the others lacked?"

I did not get the self-absorbed, rock-star answer that you might expect. Gina lifted her head up, pointed her nose ring right at me, and said, "F***ing luck."

Other people who have made it to the top note the importance of luck in achieving success, but they use a slightly different choice of words. According to Ron Gafford, CEO of Austin Industries, "We try to design careers and design businesses that are not contingent on luck. But I believe luck always plays a vital role." Stephen Lambright of Anheuser Busch agrees: "There are many successful people who, if they are honest with themselves, have to say some of this was luck." Doug Bain of Boeing agrees that success requires a lot of luck, and he listed for me some of those lucky factors: positive effects from certain matters outside of your control such as mergers, the timing of the retirement of those above you on the corporate ladder, and whether or not you have the opportunity to get exposure to senior management—to name just a few. Indeed, most of the top professionals I interviewed for this book stated without hesitation that luck played a big role in their success.

Getting Lucky

So there can be no doubt. *The invincible executive is very lucky.* That is a little disturbing. How can a self-improvement book require that the reader become "lucky"? I'll say it again in very stark terms: if you want to become an invincible executive, you have to be lucky.

The good news is that *everyone is lucky.* According to a wide array of top executives, from Dave Ruf, CEO of the international engineering firm Burns & McDonnell, to top prosecutor Ed Dowd, it is a simple law of probability that over the course of a forty- or fifty-year career, every one of us is going to have two, four, or ten very fortuitous events that occur right out of the blue in front of our very eyes. The problem is that 97 percent of us (1) don't recognize the lucky event when it occurs, (2) recognize the event but don't take advantage of the opportunity it offers, or (3) mistake unlucky events for lucky ones and make bad choices. Those who reach the top and stay there do not make these mistakes.

As Dave Ruf of Burns & McDonnell said, "There are opportunities that go past you weekly, daily, maybe even hourly. Some people recognize them and some people don't. You'd better be ready." The invincible executive is very good at recognizing real opportunity, culling out false opportunity, and then turning true opportunity into accomplishment. Most invincible executives believe that, assuming you have talent, your time will come if you are adept at recognizing opportunity. "There is a whole army of people whose job it is to find talent, and to get those people to the right jobs," says Emmy-winning producer Christopher Lloyd. "Luck might bring the guy who deserves to be a boss in there in four years instead of seven or bad luck might hold him back and he doesn't get there for twelve years . . . but if you are really talented, you're going to get found out." The key is recognizing *when the opportunity that will materialize does in fact materialize.*

Grind Your Teeth, but Bite Your Tongue

According to former Senator Bob Dole, among many others, a key quality that draws luck to a career is carefully calculated patience. Jim Parker, CEO of Southwest Airlines, stated the flip side. "Impatience is a major factor in career downfalls," he noted.

Now when top professionals say that patience is essential to success, they are not talking about passivity. Rather, they recognize that, as a matter of pure professional science, time will present opportunity, so patience is a prerequisite to success. However, there is an important distinction to make here. *Invincible executives are not patient people; they are people who are capable of being patient.*

For example, I recently saw a young executive torpedo his career by taking on a boss whom he rightfully felt to be incompetent. This boss was less than two years away from retirement; the young executive had thirty-five years left in his career. Had the young executive simply bitten his tongue and waited the situation out, a major promotion would have opened up right in front of him like the parting of the Red Sea. The young man made a fatal career error when he chose not to wait for his boss's retirement to materialize—even when he had a good idea that the event was coming. The incompetent boss had enough friends at the company to get the junior executive fired. This story illustrates the point, gleaned from the careers of both successful and unsuccessful people alike, that the poor manipulation of a potentially lucky situation usually leads to a career flameout. Conversely, the tactical use of patience opens the door to opportunity.

Now you don't have to just sit there and wait around for something lucky to happen—although that can and has worked for many people. Invincible executives do create opportunities, and you can maximize your chance for a successful career by creating opportunities. However, "opportunity creation" is a delicate process. You can never *force* an opportunity. Let's discuss the difference between forcing an opportunity and creating an opportunity.

Forcing Opportunity: The Professional Kiss of Death

First, the wrong way. The most common way people ineffectively force opportunity is through "back channeling"—a fast route to nowhere, according to senior Boeing attorney John Judy. Back channeling is going around someone you should be dealing with in order to get to someone higher up. For example, I know a young man we will call William. He was a junior aide to a U.S. senator. William was very ambitious, constantly trying to become more "visible" to very important people—his boss, other senators, senior constituents. He continuously pushed for access to top Washingtonians. His motto was, literally, "visibility is everything."

William reported to the senator's administrative assistant (AA), who is effectively the chief of staff for the senator. One day, the AA told William to write a letter for the AA's signature to a congresswoman so that the AA could report to the congresswoman what the senator planned to do about a conflict between a bill pending in the House of Representatives and one pending in the Senate. William wrote the letter, signed it himself, and then sent it to the congresswoman. Worse yet, he called the congresswoman personally to discuss it. The congresswoman politely took the call, and she and William actually resolved the matter. But she did make a tactful mention to the AA that she had been surprised that someone so junior was negotiating with her.

The AA approached William and reminded him that the AA was supposed to lead the negotiations. William then made the typical lame reply that someone confronted with his or her inappropriate back channeling always makes: I thought you were too busy and just did it myself. The result was twofold: William looked incapable of following instructions, and he came across as insincere. It did not matter that William had both increased his visibility with the congresswoman and successfully resolved the problem. His young career took a big hit.

Back channelers always follow the same route to failure—they ignore the chain of command and then lie about the reason. William was looking for a new job within three months of the incident I described above. Invincible executives get noticed by senior people by doing their jobs well; not by doing someone else's job and not by going around people to gain access to higher-ups.

Another way that misguided employees commonly force opportunities is by demanding (or simply adopting) a title or a promotion. Here is an extreme example, but it is a true story that illustrates the point well. Stephanie was an assistant facilities manager in charge of leasing office and factory space for a large manufacturing company. She was bright and very ambitious. One day her boss found a letter she had sent to the owner of a warehouse. She had signed the letter with her name, and underneath her signature was the title "Chief Facilities Officer."

She had just made up the title. Everyone at the company knew that the company did not have a chief facilities officer—and the whole department thought it sounded not only disingenuous but downright silly for someone to adopt such a stilted label for a rather modest job. Stephanie became a sort of a joke around the office after that—"Hey look, there goes the chief facilities officer!" Worse yet, the company lawyer noted, by putting the word "officer" in her title, she represented to outsiders that she had the authority of a senior company official, which could create serious liability issues in the event of a dispute. Stephanie's career never really recovered from her effort to force an opportunity.

Recognizing and Creating Opportunity: An Essential Professional Skill

Earlier, I quoted invincible executives who said that you should always focus on doing your current job well. Consistently, top executives recommended against constantly pushing for a promotion or implying that you are more than you really are. These important observations, while true, cannot be equated with the unproductive idea that you should keep your head in the sand. You can focus on doing your current job well while simultaneously taking steps to ensure that you learn of and take advantage of opportunities that will come your way. "One definition of luck is that somebody opened the door and what you look at as luck really is what you prepared for, and that is the ability to step through the door and take advantage of the situation," according to Stephen Lambright of Anheuser-Busch.

So let's discuss a very different approach to harnessing luck: recognizing and creating—rather than forcing—opportunities. There are legitimate ways to increase the likelihood that luck will come your way. You increase your odds of success if you carefully cultivate and grow your own luck. Here's how invincible executives do it.

While invincible executives do not force opportunity, they do gather as much knowledge about the greater goings-on in their company and industry as possible. They start by reading company newsletters and industry publications. This publicly available data gives them a base from which to assess possible opportunities. Several of the invincible executives I interviewed for the book had trade publications sitting on their desks—some of them had five or six. There can be no doubt that you find opportunity by staying completely on top of developments in your company and your industry.

But the process of opportunity identification and exploitation goes much further. *The invincible executive uses inside information to advance his or her career.* Remember, it is illegal to trade stock on inside information; but it is not illegal to plan your career based on inside information. Many invincible executives I interviewed told similar stories about their early years in business. They developed friendships among a wide cross section of people in their companies. They made a point to get to know the financial and accounting people in their companies. That way, they remained generally apprised of the financial health of the company, and they often knew of mergers, acquisitions, and divestments before anyone else did. These aspiring professionals also made a point of getting to know the company lawyers, and these friendships gave them inside information on big business deals in the works or serious potential liabilities that the company had to address. They also got to know the company marketing staff so that they could keep informed on the state of customer relationships.

A couple of successful executives—both on condition of anonymity—confided to me that they deliberately cultivated friendships with the executive assistants to top managers so that they could very tactfully accomplish two objectives: (1) keep tabs on what the top execs were up to and (2) learn what the top execs valued in their workers.

One of them told me this startlingly Machiavellian story—right out of *How to Succeed in Business Without Really Trying*—about the dividends yielded by getting to know the assistants to top executives. "From becoming friendly with the assistant to our executive vice president, I learned that the executive VP hated beards, detested junior executives who drove expensive foreign cars, was very macho about drinking his coffee black, loved the New York Mets but thought they needed better pitching, and was looking to replace the marketing manager on one of his pet projects. At the next meeting that I attended in his presence, I made a point of: (1) shaving my sideburns before the meeting; (2) pouring a cup of coffee before the meeting and making a smilingly derogatory remark about cream and sugar; (3) telling the executive VP in small talk before the meeting that my dream baseball team was the Mets with Roger Clemens added to the lineup; (4) casually working into the discussion at the actual meeting that one of my biggest rivals drove a BMW 700 series car that would put my Ford to shame; and finally (5) bringing up some carefully organized and presented ideas on how we could improve our marketing of the boss's favorite project. . . . I was promoted to senior marketing manager the next month and my career soared."

Yikes. How calculating can one be? For better or worse, it worked. Rather than running around telling everyone that he was really good or deserved a promotion, this man, now a top executive himself, gathered knowledge and then used it at the right time. That is creating opportunity rather than forcing it.

Four Ways to Avoid False Opportunity

I was at a party just a few days before writing this chapter, and a young woman was telling me a story about how her father had been bilked out of $3 million by a con man who claimed that he could get investors a 30 percent per year return by holding inventory for a major department store until the store could use it. The con man—who had a criminal record a mile long—allegedly bilked intelligent, wealthy people out of tens of millions of dollars before he skipped town. Similarly, one of the people I interviewed for this book had just lost $300,000 in a Ponzi scheme of a like nature. I am surprised at how many sharp people fall for schemes that are obviously too good to be true. Despite their intelligence, they have failed to distinguish between real and false opportunity.

During the course of a career, you will be presented with many "opportunities" that are fronts for disaster. You must be able to ferret out false opportunity and stay away from it. Here are a few pointers for discerning the authentic opportunities from the false ones. We'll use the example of buying a business as a metaphor for all professional opportunities.

First, be skeptical of the hard sell. Most opportunities are found through research and study, not offered up to you on a silver platter. "Success lies upstream," as Dave Ruf, CEO of Burns & McDonnell, put it. "You do not drift into it." Because amazing opportunities are snapped up fast, they are few and far between. According to an acquaintance of mine who is a midsized-business broker, "If someone, for example, offers to sell his or her business to you with glowing promises, always ask if the business has already been offered to someone else. Nine times out of ten it has, and the deal did not go through—for a very good reason."

Second, research not only the business you are acquiring, but also the people with whom you are negotiating. Determine whether they have ever declared personal bankruptcy or whether a previous business that they ran failed. Do a background check to ensure that they have no criminal record. Find out if they have ever been in trouble with consumer organizations or regulatory agencies. Do LexisNexis searches to determine if they get a lot of bad press or file lawsuits at the drop of a hat. Know not only the business, but also the people who make up the business. Often shady people associate themselves with reputable businesses to gain an aura of respectability.

Third, as Walter Metcalfe, the successful corporate lawyer mentioned in the introduction to this book, once told me, "streamline the opportunity." Determine the positives and the negatives of the project. If the positives outweigh the negatives, pursue the deal. However, do not *do the deal* unless you can still eliminate some of the negatives. That process builds in a "risk pad" in case your original assessment of the pros and cons turns out to be incorrect. If, for example, a company approaches you about a merger, it is usually because the company has determined that it cannot survive on its own. Even if you think you can turn it around, cut out some of the risks before you start trying. Transform the opportunity that you are being offered by leaving some of the downsides on the cutting room floor. Maybe you do not take the whole company; maybe you do not take all of the people; maybe you demand that the offering company insure its more shaky receivables. Even when a transaction looks pretty good, you need to take a couple of steps to streamline the deal such that you tilt the odds even more toward success from your standpoint. You do this by putting some risk pads or downside backstops into the deal.

Fourth, do not become giddy and careless when a real opportunity presents itself. Often in the excitement of getting a good deal done, people become sloppy and convert the opportunity into a problem. They do not want to address potential negative developments for fear of throwing a wet blanket on the opportunity that has presented itself. For example, I know a man who sold his business to a Fortune 500 company in exchange for a 20 percent interest in a partnership through which the big company would run his business. The big company sneaked into the purchase contract a buyout provision that gave the big company the "sole discretion" to value and purchase my acquaintance's 20 percent interest at any time. Within a year, the company announced that it had valued his interest at less than $100,000 and tried to buy him out. An independent expert valued his interest at over $20 million. My acquaintance had to go through a big lawsuit to get a fair settlement, and even then the sum he got was below the market value of the company. He had been so swept up with the idea of being bought out by a big conglomerate—which was in fact the opportunity of a lifetime—that he became careless with the details.

The concept of taking specific measures that reduce downside risk is essential to the process of taking advantage of fortuitous professional developments. For example, top executive recruiters always insist that their clients get predetermined, written severance packages before taking new jobs, even where the previous holders of the jobs did not have such contracts. This is just another form of "downside backstop."

When the positives outweigh the negatives, you have an opportunity. But do not take the opportunity until you can whittle away a few more of the negatives. Then do not get so giddy that you become careless in documenting the transaction.

Remember That Problems Often Present the Greatest Opportunities

The accurate observation that you must whittle away the negative aspects of opportunities cannot be confused with the inaccurate idea that opportunities only arise during good times. In fact, many career-making opportunities have arisen during troubled times. "It seems to be a common theme among successful people," according to Drew Baur, the chairman of Southwest Bank and an owner of the St. Louis Cardinals baseball team. "They don't cower in times of turmoil. Rather, they look around and say, 'How can I turn this around to my advantage, to the advantage of the people who work for me?'"

Mike Sears, the executive vice president and CFO of Boeing, used to work for McDonnell-Douglas. In the mid-1990s the CEO of McDonnell-Douglas sent him to Long Beach, California, to head up the commercial airliner division of McDonnell. Within a few months, Mr. Sears determined that the commercial airliner division of the company would be unable to compete over the long term with Airbus and Boeing. He reported his findings honestly to the CEO. Those findings contributed to the decision of McDonnell to merge with Boeing—a move that strengthened Boeing and saved the legacy of McDonnell. It also had the effect of cementing Sears's reputation as a straight shooter who is not afraid to identify a problem and participate in developing creative, daring, and controversial solutions.

Sears's coworker, Doug Bain, whom we met earlier, described to me a defining moment in his career—when he agreed to lead a difficult negotiation with the Boeing labor union in 1986. Rather than shy away from controversy, Bain recognized the negotiation as an opportunity to show his ability to work under pressure. When the negotiations concluded successfully, people at the top of the company took notice and that one incident changed his entire career trajectory.

"Problems create opportunities" is a motto of Sam Fox, a phenomenally successful and wealthy Midwestern entrepreneur who has acquired 131 manufacturing companies through a holding company known as the Harbour Group. In the 1970s, he realized that American business schools were almost totally focused on finance, marketing, and investment banking. They were ignoring manufacturing, and there was little fresh talent in the manufacturing sector. Consequently, manufacturing expertise in the United States was falling behind that of Germany and Japan. So Fox, who is an experienced manufacturing executive, organized a company to bring modern manufacturing know-how to "Rust Belt" companies. He assembled a staff of seasoned executives in various manufacturing disciplines and began purchasing manufacturing companies. Fox now has a fortune estimated to be in the hundreds of millions of dollars.

Many senior corporate executives told me stories about how their careers actually benefited during a wave of mergers and downsizing initiatives at their companies. Remember, they note, when a company is under stress, the normally rigid corporate structure becomes more fluid. Most people hunker down and brace for the worst. Bad idea. Instead of lying low and trying to hold on to what you've got, look for opportunities. To do so, according to Norma Clayton of Boeing, "You go into the merger situation without any preconceptions about what is going to happen. You stay out of the politics and you listen. You watch the feet of the people who are making the decisions. And you look for the opportunity."

In order to maximize these opportunities, volunteer to work on "transition teams" that effectuate mergers; and make lateral moves out of "redundant" areas like marketing and accounting and into areas that the company perceives to be most attractive to potential merger partners—the bestselling product line, the areas of the company that utilize the most sophisticated intellectual property. The invincible executive always converts institutional problems into personal opportunities in these creative and incisive ways.

RULE

5

Promote the Organization, Not Yourself

📷 **SNAPSHOT**

Do you actively seek personal recognition through self-promotion?

Yes: 28 percent **No:** 72 percent

The question of self-promotion is a tricky one—and one about which there is less of a consensus than in other areas I investigated. There are a number of highly successful CEOs and top professionals who are shameless self-promoters. In business, Donald Trump and Hugh Hefner come to mind. In the legal arena, F. Lee Bailey and Johnny Cochran seem to fit the same bill. Don King, the boxing promoter, has publicly acknowledged and demonstrated (about a million times) that self-promotion is a very important part of his professional identity.

But not all self-promoters are flamboyant showmen like Donald Trump and Don King. Even the sincere, mild-mannered top medical researcher, Dr. Joshua Korzenik, acknowledged that in the field of medical research, self-promotion is critical because one key to success is getting grant money. And the art of "grantsmanship," as Dr. Korzenik puts it, necessarily involves a degree of self-promotion—as distasteful as it is to him. In fact, a sizeable percentage—over a quarter—of the people I interviewed for this book confided to me—some off the record—that self-promotion is an important part of professional success.

On the other hand, many top executives shun the spotlight and dislike those who seek it. "Those who promote themselves have got a strike against them even if they are good at what they do," says Sam Fox, the low-key owner of the Harbour Group, whom I discussed above. "Because the question becomes: Who is this guy, who is he really looking out for? Is he a fighter pilot looking out for himself, or is he a team player with the company's interests at heart?" Fox asks. Richard Bell, the longtime CEO of the highly successful international engineering firm HDR, Inc., puts it even more bluntly: "Self-promotion is a dead end. It destroys you. It destroys the opportunity that could be in front of you." Others who seem to fall into the camp of top executives who shun self-promotion include the late Sam Walton, the founder of Wal-Mart, and Ken Chenault, the CEO of American Express.

So what is the answer? There is a way to reconcile the apparent conflict between those who favor self-promotion and those who reject it. Let's analyze the situation in greater detail.

Only Owners and Founders Get Away with Self-Promotion

To understand the relationship between self-promotion and professional success, I went to one of the great anomalies I know in the business world, Jack Schmitt. He owns an impressive collection of automobile dealerships across Southern Illinois—Ford, Chevrolet,

Nissan, Cadillac, you name it—the annual sales of which were $168 million in 2001. Yet, after more than forty years in the car business, he has never one time appeared in the thousands of television commercials for his dealerships—probably a first for an auto dealer.

I asked Jack about the importance of self-promotion in business, and he made a few valuable observations, which were echoed in whole or in part by many of the other top executives I interviewed. First, according to Jack, the only people who can get away with extensive self-promotion are those who founded and/or own their own businesses. If you own the company, those who depend upon you for their income will always encourage you to promote yourself. In fact, it is common wisdom among business owners that sooner or later your advertising agency is going to recommend that you, the owner (or your children), should appear in the television commercials promoting the company. It is always the safe route for outsiders to tell the owner that he or she or the owner's beautiful daughter should be on television. It strokes the owner's ego and it eliminates the need for more creative approaches to selling the product or service.

One ad executive told me—on condition of anonymity, for obvious reasons—that he deliberately crafted an ad campaign about a dog when he learned that his client and the client's wife were childless, but they were almost religiously devoted to their poodle. The ad executive told the owner about the dog idea and then let the client come up with the idea to cast his poodle as the dog in the campaign. So, sure, you see a lot of business owners engaged in blatant acts of self-promotion.

But is it really the route to the top? Not usually. Jack Schmitt noted that employees and customers generally react with smiling indifference to a business owner who constantly self-promotes. People laugh at the stories of Hugh Hefner appearing on camera every ten minutes in a bathrobe surrounded by three girlfriends with a combined age less than his, and they snicker at Donald Trump staging publicity stunts at just about every public event that he can. If you act like that, you get nicknames like "The Donald" but no one really hates you for it. Overt self-promotion by business founders and owners does not really help the business, but it doesn't hurt either. It is just a silly ego trip for the boss and his or her family.

Schmitt notes that if, on the other hand, you do not own your business—even if you are the CEO—the owners and the board of directors to whom you report will look less kindly on self-promotion. By plastering your own picture all over magazines or television, you appear to put your personal interests above those of the entity—a perception that has cost thousands of talented people their careers. This principle applies not only to CEOs, but to mid-level executives as well. If you are constantly trying to get in the company newsletter or take credit for a company success, those around you will resent the efforts you have made to be in the spotlight. The resentment will build to a point where people secretly hope that you fall from your perch, and, in those circumstances, no one will lift a finger to help you if you encounter some professional trouble.

In the case of professionals (as opposed to business owners or corporate employees), self-promotion can get you some notoriety, but often the process backfires miserably. For example, you frequently see publicity-hound lawyers on CNN. Check the court records and you will find that judges skewer them in court on a regular basis. The judges hold all the cards in litigation, and, as one federal judge recently confided to me, they often feel the need to put haughty celebrity lawyers in their place to remind them that the court of law and the court of the media are two very different places. As part of my research for this book, I studied court opinions relating to cases handled by a couple of celebrity lawyers, and found that these lawyers have lost an average of 75 percent of their cases in the last five years—statistical confirmation of the anecdotes that judges and lawyers have given me. *Publicity is like a fire— bright and flashy, but difficult to contain and capable of consuming you.*

Becoming the Conduit for the Organization

Based upon the observations of Jack Schmitt and others, it would seem that self-promotion is not usually a means to professional invincibility and often sows the seeds of failure. But here is where the tension lies. Not less than ten of the top executives I interviewed said words to the effect that "you cannot be successful unless people know you are doing a good job." Many competent people toil away in oblivion because others get credit for their successes. That leads to a simple question: how can you make your accomplishments known without becoming a despised self-promoter?

The answer is "entity embodiment." Several CEOs and CFOs told me that you have to become the symbol of the organization. You do not promote yourself; rather, you are chosen to represent the talents, abilities, and accomplishments of the company or organization as a whole. For example, both William C. Ford Jr. and August Busch IV are featured prominently in advertising campaigns for their companies. They of course can get away with it because their families founded the business. But, more important, they use their platform to discuss the history and heritage of their companies, the processes by which their products are made, and the importance of the people who work there. They come across as low-key, soft-spoken, and very modest spokespeople for the product and the people whom they embody. They are not promoting themselves; they have become symbols of their companies. That is the critical difference between a successful self-promoter and an unsuccessful one.

This philosophy applies to everyone else who aspires to be a top manager or professional. People who are the driving force behind a company's success always ensure that they are the spokesperson through whom the success is recognized, but they never mention themselves. They always give credit to others—particularly their bosses, according to leading banker and St. Louis Cardinals owner Drew Baur. They mention their company name often when interviewed. They freely refer to others in the organization—often giving them more credit than they really deserve. "They substitute the word 'we' for the word 'me' wherever possible," as Congressman Richard Gephardt put it.

The person giving the credit to others always benefits the most because that person (1) delivers the message and (2) ingratiates himself or herself to others by giving them credit. As long as you visualize yourself as the embodiment of the positive aspects of your company, you will naturally become the center of attention and will never have to force the issue with overt self-promotion.

Similarly, effective self-promoters never develop protective relationships with customers, clients, or suppliers, according to Bill Stowers, a top Boeing vice president in charge of managing hundreds of supplier relationships. Rather, they manage a relationship between their company and the other companies. For example, they volunteer to participate in training and presentations, to organize joint marketing sessions and award ceremonies, and they use these opportunities to introduce other employees of their company to the customer.

Norma Clayton, the top Boeing official we met earlier, never sits at the head of the table in a meeting with customers, suppliers, or the people who report to her. "In fact, I always lower my chair down a level," she said, so that her head is below everyone else's. They know she is the boss, so she uses these tactics to create better "transparency and dialogue" during her meetings. Earl Graves, the publisher of *Black Enterprise* magazine and a member of the board of directors of several major companies, also said that he will not sit at the head of a table during a meeting. That makes him more a part of the "entity," not an island of authority.

"You want to be the switching station that gets information and people from your company to theirs and vice versa; but you can never become a roadblock or the tension within your organization will build until that block is broken—usually at your expense," says Jack Schmitt. "I call it 'flipping the M.' Turn the Me into We, and that kind of self-promotion is just fine."

What you cannot do, confirms Doug Bain of Boeing, is "talk about yourself and take credit for the team." That approach might make you feel like you are doing well, but ultimately it will shorten your career, according to Bain—among others. They all agree that self-promoters can do well at the lower and middle rungs of the organization because standing out is half the battle. Once the spotlight turns to you, however, you better be a team player all the way. "If your actions are good enough, people will notice them, and they will not need your embellishment and your constant spin on them," Bain adds.

The Community Proxy

Finally, banker Drew Baur notes that most successful executives become best known not for their on-the-job accomplishments, but for their involvement with the community. They participate in charities and fund-raisers. This commitment "cannot be hollow," but must be sincere, according to Baur. Indeed, Baur believes it is the duty of business professionals to take an active role in their communities. He notes, however, that civic activities have the secondary benefit of increasing your standing in the business community.

The Hollywood Rule of Self-Promotion

Joel Gotler, the Beverly Hills agent I discussed earlier, belongs to the sizeable minority of top executives who believe that self-promotion is almost always good for a career. And in Hollywood, he may be right. But even Mr. Gotler and Hollywood have one limit on the extent to which you can successfully self-promote: never become bigger than the client.

When I interviewed Adam Clymer, Washington correspondent for the *New York Times*, he said effectively the same thing: the reporter should never be bigger than the story. In media-centered fields like music, movies, and journalism, you can get away with more overtly self-promotional activity (jeez, look at Geraldo), but you cross the line when your self-promotion "diminishes the product," "becomes the story," or "overshadows the client." Good advice from the pro-promotion side of the court.

6

Connections Get You a First Chance, but Never a Second One

📷 **SNAPSHOT**

How important are connections and networking to professional success?

Important: 25 percent   **Unimportant:** 75 percent

A management consultant told me the following story, which captures in a nutshell the value of networking and connections to professional success. The CEO of a major company called the chairman of a prominent consulting firm. The consulting firm received an average of $4 million annually from the company that the CEO ran. The CEO asked the firm's chairman to "consider" his son for an associate's position at the consulting firm. The son had a grade point average of 3.0 and a class rank of 64 out of 150 at a midranked business school. The consulting firm normally hired students from that business school only if they were in the top 10 percent of their class.

The chairman of the consulting firm was concerned that the firm could lose the company as a client unless he hired the CEO's son. He recommended to the recruiting committee that the firm lower its standards and hire the kid. There was stiff resistance to hiring him among some members of the recruiting committee, but other members of the recruiting committee did a lot of consulting work for that client and sided with the chairman. The young man got the offer.

Within six months, the young man had screwed up two projects and treated a client rudely. The consulting firm lost one client, fired the kid, and lost the father's business as well. The partners who had recommended against hiring the kid were merciless on those who had supported the hiring.

"If we had just told the CEO that his son simply did not meet our threshold requirements for associates—in very straight and objective terms—the kid would have been better off, our clients would have been happier, our partnership would have been wealthier, and we might not have lost the father's company as a client. That was the last time we played the connections game," the consultant lamented.

Connection Defined

I have read and heard more opining about the value of "networking" and "connections" than I could relate in an entire book. But, having discussed the issue with people who made it big and who themselves are now the "connection" that everyone covets, two pretty cut-and-dried principles emerge. First, connections might get you in the door. Second, they will never keep you in the room.

Bill Shaw, president and chief operating officer of Marriott International, summed up the views of many of the people I interviewed when he said that "connections" are of very limited value in the corporate world. "They might open a door—maybe help you get an interview—but they will rarely get you a job or a promotion," according to Shaw. Most invincible executives feel that aspiring professionals place too much importance upon connections and networking.

That said, they do agree, as Shaw said, that a connection can get someone in the door of an organization. Even to get in the door, however, you need to have a "true" connection. Let's start our discussion, therefore, with the definition of a "connection." Just as you cannot fabricate opportunity; you cannot fabricate a connection. Remember, prominent people are inundated with requests for help. And it seems that the vast majority of them will help when they can.

Yet there are very important limits. First, former Attorney General Janet Reno says that she very much dislikes being asked to write a recommendation for someone she does not know well. Here is how she put it: "'Ms. Reno, would you write me a letter of recommendation?' 'I'm sorry, my dear, I don't know your name, what you do, or anything about you.' 'Oh, I thought you might just churn something out for me. It would mean so much to me.' And I say, 'Well, have I had any experience with your work?' 'No.' 'Well sorry.'"

Former United States Attorney Edward L. Dowd Jr. similarly notes that he is always willing to take the time to recommend or otherwise assist someone *whom he knows.* "I help someone out with a job recommendation literally every week and I am happy to do so," he says. What he is reluctant to do is recommend someone he has never heard of just because he or she is the friend of a friend. "First, it never works," he says. "People can tell a generic recommendation when they see it and it carries no weight, so it is a waste of everyone's time." Second, you must remember that credibility is a very valuable commodity among invincible executives. "This guy

I am supposed to rave about may be a total loser. I'll look like an idiot recommending him," says Dowd.

If you are seeking a connection through a friend, it may sometimes be possible for you to arrange a meeting with the connection and provide that person materials demonstrating your accomplishments. "That works sometimes, but it is still a long shot," says Dowd. "Unless you can say 'I have known and worked with this person,' letters of recommendation usually get thrown in the trash."

Connection Etiquette

Next, there is a pretty well-established etiquette for using connections. You can never appear opportunistic in cultivating a connection. For example, producer Christopher Lloyd acknowledges that connections open doors in Hollywood. You cannot dispute it. He has helped many young writers along in their careers. However, what never works—and will actually backfire—is to appear opportunistic. Lloyd related to me a story about a pickup basketball league that he played in a few years back. One day after the game, one of the players, whom Lloyd hardly knew, handed him a script as he was walking to his car after the game. Reflecting on the limited interaction that they had previously, Lloyd perceived that this person may have joined the league just to get access to him. It all looked very contrived. Lloyd chose not to read the script.

Another important piece of "connection etiquette" is that you should never overplay the relationship that you have with a connection. For example, I had an acquaintance who repeatedly told me how chummy he was with a congressman. As luck would have it, we were both at a fund-raiser that the congressman attended, so I asked the acquaintance to introduce me to the congressman.

Appearing very nervous, the acquaintance approached the congressman. The conversation went something like this.

Acquaintance: Hello, Congressman, let me introduce you to my friend, Tom Schweich.

Congressman: Tom, good to meet you.

He shook my hand. Then he turned to my acquaintance.

Congressman: I think we've met before, haven't we?

Acquaintance: Sure Congressman, you remember, on the food irradiation bill.

Congressman: Yeah, sure, I remember. Well it's good to see you again.

Acquaintance: How is Susan these days?

Congressman: Susan who?

Acquaintance: Your wife.

Congressman: Oh, Suzanne. She is doing great. She loves being a grandmother. You know, all the fun, none of the work.

Acquaintance: Yeah, my parents are the same way.

Congressman: Well, ah . . . friend . . . good to catch up with you.

It was pretty clear to me that the congressman had no clue who my acquaintance was and had only played along to save face for him. Moral: do not overplay your connections or you will look like a total idiot.

Finally, you get the most out of a connection when you sincerely want to learn from the person whose help you are seeking. Songwriter and recording artist Sheryl Crow told me that she has no problem at all with the idea of using connections to help a career along. But there is one big caveat: you have to have sincere intentions. "When I went to L.A., I used every connection I could possibly find," Crow told me. "But I enjoyed the *process* of learning from these people. And I think if you approach it like that—not using people to get somewhere but just fitting into the process—who can I learn from, who can help me to become better—doors will fly open. I think everything has to do with intention. When your intentions are pure, that is honored by the universe."

Pat Finneran, a top executive at Boeing, echoes Ms. Crow's sentiments. He does not like the idea of a pure "connection." Rather, he in his career has had mentors, like former Treasury Secretary and White House Chief of Staff Don Regan, who at times gave him advice. The invincible executive, therefore—according to top professionals ranging from songwriters to defense contractors—does not sit around plotting how to use a connection to get somewhere. Rather, he or she has flexible goals and takes the opportunity to learn from people who have reached similar goals. Those people can detect that honest enthusiasm and will naturally offer to help their aspiring friend along with his or her career.

Make It Their Idea

One way to ensure that you do not look opportunistic when asking someone to help you is to make the assistance the other person's idea. Instead of dumping a script on someone you barely know, go out for a beer with him or her a couple of times. Use less formal settings to let the person know your aspirations, and seek legitimate advice from that person. If the person likes you and perceives that you are sincere and talented, he or she may offer to help you. It often works like a charm. Take it from Lloyd and Crow—two of the top people in their respective entertainment fields—the best connections are those built around friendship, trust, and sincerity—not by desperately throwing your request at someone during a fleeting or contrived opportunity.

Do Not Waste Too Much Time Networking

Let's discuss a term closely related to connections. Most invincible executives agree that "networking"—the formal, planned, and deliberate cultivation of relationships for the purpose of assisting one's career—is also of very limited value in getting jobs or promotions. This belief is consistent with my personal experience. As a lawyer who works for a firm that represents a large percentage of the large companies in my region, I get frequent networking requests. For example, an acquaintance of mine decided to close his small, floundering ad agency. He proudly told me that he was going to embark on a massive "networking campaign" to try to get a new job. I set him up with a couple of my friends. From what he told me, he must have taken forty people or more out to lunch to pursue leads for a marketing job. He was a firm believer in the power of networking.

About seven months later, he called me with the good news. He had finally landed a job as the director of marketing for a hotel. I congratulated him and asked, "Which one of your lunches paid off?"

"Actually, I got the job by responding to a want ad," he replied.

This is not an uncommon scenario. Invincible executives generally believe that mid-level executives waste too much time networking. While being a member of a trade association is, for example, good for perspective on your industry, it rarely leads to a new job. Or, as Doug Bain of Boeing put it, "I think you are not going to get to the top of an organization unless the people at the top know you because you have fulfilled whatever expectations they have or skills they want. But you have to separate that from the 'schmoozing.' I don't think those connections do you a bit of good. I remember that I mentored a young executive in the contracts department. She kept emphasizing 'networking' and I finally said, 'Knock off the networking.' If your networking is part of the job you are doing [like marketing or community relations], that is great. But if all you are doing is networking in the sense of sucking up, that works against you."

The Payback Connection

Another blunt insight: *"The best connections are payback connections,"* a top Republican fund-raiser once told me. She explained that as you seek your connection to a particular job or assignment that you want, you must understand the relationship between the connection and the "connectee." The connectee is the person who ultimately makes the decision to give you the job or the assignment for which you are using the connection. If the connection is soliciting a "favor" from the connectee on your behalf, then your chances of success in using that connection are better than nothing, but less than 25 percent, according to this fund-raiser. On the other hand, if you become the chip that represents a "payback" for something that the connection did for the connectee, "your odds shoot up to about 80 percent," she told me.

A novelist, whom we'll call Jimmy, related this story to me. Jimmy's agent was shopping around Jimmy's very first manuscript. The agent liked the novel. After three readings with prominent editors, however, the agent had no takers. So the agent called an editor at a leading publishing house who owed the agent a big favor. Years earlier, this editor was toiling in oblivion until the agent handed him a great novel by an established author looking for a new publisher. Unsurprisingly, the novel did well and it put the editor on the map.

"Now it is payback time," said Jimmy's agent, handing the editor Jimmy's manuscript. "I gave you a great author when you had nothing; now I want you to take a nothing author who I believe has talent." The deal closed the next week. The first novel did so-so, but the second one did better, and the novelist's career soon took off. Jimmy's agent had demanded a payback, not a favor. The lesson: make sure if possible that the decision maker owes something to the connection, and make sure that you become the payback chip by learning as much about the relationship between the connection and the connectee as possible.

Juanita Hinshaw, CFO of the multibillion-dollar electrical giant Graybar, candidly acknowledges that "when you have used connections you have to be willing to be used. So I've let it be a two-way street." In those instances, therefore, where a connection can be helpful, try to be the "payback." It greatly increases your odds of success.

Connections Evaporate the Moment You Walk in the Door

When the Bush administration was formulating its energy policy in 2001, Vice President Cheney solicited the advice of senior Enron executives. They were big contributors to the Republican cause. Enron had a major league connection, and it no doubt assisted Enron in getting some pro–oil industry points in the final draft of the policy. Few could dispute that a key connection got Enron chairman Kenneth Lay in the most powerful door in the world—the White House door.

But even a connection that powerful could not buy Mr. Lay a cup of coffee when the energy giant began to implode. Enron's calls for help from the White House fell on deaf ears. "They dropped him like a hot potato," a columnist noted. The reason: connections will never get you a second chance. They will never rescue you from a screwup. They provide access but *no staying power whatsoever*. Once you have attained the position for which you used the connection, you have to succeed on your own merits. Just like the kid who got the job at the accounting firm. Even a father who was a powerful client could not rescue him from his misdeeds.

Affirmative Action Versus Connection

Affirmative action is a state-sanctioned "connection"—a way to get in the door for those not fortunate enough to have traditional connections. Most members of minorities with whom I have discussed the issue believe that anyone who can benefit from affirmative action should take maximum advantage of the opportunity and not feel guilty about it at all.

"Country clubs, private high schools, and the connections that come out of them are like affirmative action for underachieving white people," a black judge told me on condition of anonymity. He marveled at how some Americans object to affirmative action on the grounds that it allegedly gets unqualified minorities into top jobs. He believes that the "old boy network" is the oldest form of affirmative action—and the worst form of affirmative action because it operates almost completely independent of intelligence or ability. "How many rich white fathers got their dumb sons good jobs while laughing it up with friends on a golf course?" he wondered. "Affirmative action generally overcomes disparities in educational opportunity, not disparities in intelligence. But connections can even overcome disparities in intelligence," he added.

This is an important point that all of us should keep in mind when we play a connection. There can be a backlash, and the doors will close quickly if you are not up to the task. People are watching you—many of them resentfully—and they are waiting for you to fail as soon as you play the connection card. So you can use a connection to get into the door, but the standard by which your performance is measured after that may be higher than if you had never used the connection at all.

7

When You Suffer a Setback, Come Clean and Bounce Back

┌─ 📷 **SNAPSHOT** ────────────────────────────────────┐

Have you ever suffered a serious career setback?

Yes: 70 percent   **No:** 30 percent

└──┘

Almost a third of the invincible executives I know have never suffered a career setback. They are the golden women and men of the professional world. You probably know a couple of them. They make you sick. Unfortunately, you cannot plan to be that fortunate. Just as everyone has a few lucky opportunities in his or her professional life, most of us will find ourselves in a very bad situation or two as well. In fact, three of the people I interviewed for this book suffered professional setbacks since the interview and were back on track in short order.

Invincible executives minimize the effects of setbacks by (1) coming clean and (2) bouncing back. The analysis, however, proceeds better in reverse order, so we'll start our discussion with bouncing back.

The Career Shift

In November of 2000, ultraconservative Missouri Senator John Ashcroft became the first senator ever to lose an election to a dead person. Ashcroft's opponent, Missouri Governor Mel Carnahan, had died tragically in a plane crash just a few weeks before the election. Carnahan's name remained on the ballot, however, and he won by a slim margin. The lieutenant governor appointed Governor Carnahan's wife, Jean, to be U.S. senator.

Democrats gleefully declared that Ashcroft—having now lost to a deceased person—had no political future. Four months later, however, Ashcroft was the attorney general of the United States—the senior law enforcement officer in the country and the senior advisor to the president on the critical issue of judicial nominations. As attorney general, Ashcroft found himself in an even greater position to advance a conservative agenda than he was while a senator. How did Ashcroft bounce back so quickly?

For starters, "He did not get mad at his setback," an adviser of his told me. Ashcroft had legitimate grounds to challenge the results of the Senate election he lost on two bases. First, he had a pretty good argument under Missouri law that a deceased person could not be a "resident" of the state and, therefore, could not run for Senate. Even more interesting, Ashcroft knew that the polls in the heavily Democratic areas of St. Louis had stayed open longer than provided for under the law. Against the advice of many—and very much in contrast to the strategy employed by Vice President Al Gore at the same time—Ashcroft decided not to challenge the results of the election. "It would just look like sour grapes," Ashcroft reportedly said.

Ashcroft, who was not known for having a particularly laid-back demeanor while a senator, displayed remarkable restraint in defeat. His gracious attitude seriously defused the image he had among Democrats as a doctrinaire extremist, and greatly *enhanced* his stature, even among those who disliked his conservative viewpoints.

Next, Ashcroft did not wallow in self-pity. He didn't get mad *and he didn't get sad*, a friend of his noted. Rather, he realized that "bad situations create the best opportunities," as manufacturing guru Sam Fox puts it. Ashcroft knew that, having lost a close Senate election and taken that loss gracefully, he was now one of the most high-profile unemployed Republicans in the country—this at a time when the new Republican administration had a lot of jobs to fill. So his supporters launched a grassroots campaign to get him named attorney general, and it worked. Had Ashcroft won the Senate election, the Bush administration might have been reluctant to yank a sitting Republican out of the Senate and into the Cabinet. Had Ashcroft challenged his Senate election results and lost, the Bush administration would have had trouble getting him confirmed because the election challenge would have looked too much like the Gore-Lieberman approach to the presidential election. By losing, accepting the loss, and recognizing the major *opportunity* that the loss created, Senator Ashcroft became Attorney General Ashcroft.

Making the Most of a Layoff

Stephen, the sixty-one-year-old president of a major manufacturing company, got the word that he either had to retire or lose his job. His company had been bought by a larger company, and the new owners wanted to put their own people in senior management positions. Stephen's staff was outraged. He had performed well in the job and everyone knew it. Stephen was tempted to just pick up and leave.

But Stephen was an invincible executive. He did not storm out. He did not head for Hawaii. Rather, he told the new owners that he wanted to retire from his company in sixty days. He used those sixty days to negotiate a new job with a very large competitor of the new owner. After forty-five days, he announced that he would retire as president of the old company, but that he would become a senior vice president of the larger competitor. The new owners of his old company—who had failed to get a "noncompete agreement" from Stephen or any of his top managers—were outraged, but there was nothing that they could do about the situation.

Less than two years later, Stephen's new company bought his old company. Stephen volunteered to assist in the integration of the two companies. Imagine the looks on the faces of the men who had fired him when Stephen chaired the first integration team meeting. Now Stephen held their fate in his hands.

How to Make the Shift

There are a lot of metaphors for career progress and career setbacks. In my lectures, I like comparing managing your career to being a new driver in a stick shift car. The shifting is the tough part. Since most careers have only a few major changes, none of us ever gets really good at shifting gears.

Invincible executives do not necessarily shift smoothly, but they accomplish their shifts successfully. Here is how they seem to do it. First, they sense when it is time to make a major career shift. They know when they cannot sustain their current momentum in the job that they have now. Indeed, there will likely be two or three times in your career when you sense that you are running out of room to operate in the current gear. You have to be attuned enough to what is going on around you in your organization to know when you are in that situation (we'll discuss how to do that a little later). When you determine that you are at the limit of the current position that you are in, you have two options. One, you can hit the brakes so that you can continue in your current gear. That is the equivalent of resigning yourself to a plateau in your career—deciding that there are more important things in life than progressing professionally. That is fine, but it means never becoming the invincible executive. You then become focused on protecting what you have.

Your other choice is to try to work the clutch to shift into the next higher level. That brief period of time when you are at the end of the capability of your current gear and are contemplating how and when to use the clutch is the time when career setbacks are most likely. You might go into overdrive; you might grind the gears; you might have a halting, sputtering transition into the next gear.

For example, you may not get the promotion that you wanted. You are all revved up; the organization isn't taking advantage of the RPMs that you are offering. It can be devastating. Or you may grind the gears a little as you move to a new job—as occurred with Ashcroft. You may not time the switch perfectly, which can mean a period of unemployment or a tense situation on the job. When you are grinding, it is an awful feeling of being neither here nor there, and suffering for it.

There may be economic or corporate circumstances beyond your control that change the direction of your career. For example, a software executive told me about the time he decided to move to a new company and immediately learned that the company had been unable to raise the money it expected to raise to continue its start-up operation. Within two weeks of his starting on the job, it was unclear if the company would have the cash to survive. The executive saw this setback as an opportunity. He jumped right into the middle of the matter and used his credibility with lenders to assist the company in finding new sources of financing. He was CEO two years later, and the company is still doing well.

When invincible executives make difficult gear shifts, they are driven by their commitment to change to a higher gear rather than slow down. That thought allows them to suppress unproductive, even self-destructive, conduct. The only option is to consider the pending or actual setback as an opportunity to *improve* the situation. Don't try just to hold on to what you have; look for the way to move ahead.

Knowing When to Shift

What you cannot allow to happen in the process is what happens to so many first-time drivers of stick shift cars—failure to make the shift. During a tough transition to a higher gear, the opportunity to make the proper adjustments to get into the higher gear lasts for a *very brief period of time.* The key, therefore, to avoiding the catastrophe is remaining coolheaded and thinking quickly. Consequently, you cannot let your emotions control the situation. Sadness, madness, frustration, and self-pity will all but ensure that you end up on the side of the road calling Triple A. Rather, you have to look at the setback simply as notice of an opportunity to improve and a challenge to your character to remain levelheaded enough to find the opportunity that will in fact present itself.

Being unemotional does not, therefore, mean being laid-back. In the examples above, both Steve and the attorney general moved very rapidly and with a sense of urgency. As Joe Ryan, executive vice president of Marriott, says, you must "deal with crisis quickly" or the situation will soon be out of your control. He recommends that you have a forty-eight-hour plan when a crisis hits your company or your career. You address the crisis with a solid plan of action within forty-eight hours—at the expense of everything else in your life for that brief period of time when you are switching gears. Invincible executives do not take sabbaticals to decide what to do with the rest of their lives. When you are in that state of limbo between gears, therefore, remember: (1) you *will* improve your situation; and (2) you are going to do it now.

Two-thirds of the invincible executives with whom I discussed the issue can point to a time in their careers when a setback led to a new and better path. Your job is to keep your emotions in check and find those opportunities. You will be amazed at how often better situations arise out of setbacks in a current position that has run its course. There is almost a sort of magic to the timing of it all, many invincible executives have said and proven.

A Cover-Up Lasts Forever . . . or Until You Get Caught

As I conducted interviews for this book, I also spoke to a couple of white-collar criminals, on condition of anonymity. They are at the other extreme from the invincible executive. Both men had very successful careers—one in government, the other in the insurance and investment business. Both of them went to prison for covering up the frauds of their organizations.

One of them made a statement that sets the tone for our discussion to follow: "A mistake takes only a moment. An admission of that mistake has repercussions that may last for a few weeks. A cover-up lasts for a lifetime, and a conviction brands you and your family forever."

I asked about twenty invincible executives this question: "What are the qualities that cause talented people to fail?" Most of them put this answer at the top of their list: failure to take responsibility for their own actions or actions of their organization. "The mistake they make is not admitting their mistakes," says Lieutenant General John Sams, former commander of the Fifteenth Air Force. "It is not the fact that you made a mistake that is important. It is how you react after you've made the mistake," General Sams adds. Most important, the general concludes, "Don't let someone else be the one who reports your mistakes." If you let others bring your errors to the attention of decision makers, they will perceive you as cowardly and devious. Executives with staying power know that they can survive a mistake if they come clean with it quickly. They also know that they will not survive if they try to cover up a mistake and get caught.

Let's look at history for the proof. President Nixon resigned because he *covered up* the Watergate scandal. Had he gone public with the information he knew about the 1972 break-in at the headquarters of the Democratic National Committee, Nixon would have been criticized for a few weeks for not controlling his people better. It would have blown over. He would have probably gone down as one of the best presidents of the twentieth century. President Clinton was impeached because he *covered up* the affair with an intern. Had the president just admitted the problem, he would have taken some heat, but his legacy would have survived in much better shape.

In 2002, Arthur Andersen imploded not because of the advice it gave Enron, but because it destroyed documents related to that advice—another cover-up. Countless other companies—Columbia Health Care, Global Crossing, etc.—have gone under or taken huge financial hits in the past two years because of accounting or billing scandals. The vast majority of the executives whose careers were ruined by these scandals had no direct role in the shady practices. Rather, they participated in cover-ups once they learned of the practices, and they got caught.

The Waco scandal that consumed conspiracy theorists in the late 1990s arose because FBI agents covered up their use of pyrotechnic tear gas on the Branch Davidians in 1993. The FBI did not cause the fire that killed the Davidians. Rather, the FBI was embarrassed that its agents had used a small amount of pyrotechnic tear gas that supporters of the Davidians *might incorrectly claim* caused the fire that killed eighty-four people. So certain agents and other officials lied about it for years—to Congress, to lawyers for the Davidians, and to the media—and they lost all credibility when the truth came out. They also seriously damaged the public perception of law enforcement through their pointless and unsuccessful cover-up. Waco Special Counsel John Danforth, an Episcopal priest, put it best in his report to the Justice Department when he said, "The failure to disclose information, more than anything else, is responsible for the loss of public faith. . . . The only antidote to public distrust is . . . openness and candor. . . . Playing it close to the line is not acceptable behavior."

The image of the Catholic Church has been tarnished badly in recent years by a terrible sex scandal. But the news focuses on high-level church officials—some of them cardinals—who knew about the problem and covered it up. The cover-up has ruined the reputations of senior church officials who honored their personal vows but covered up the misdeeds of others. In the minds of many, the cover-up is the most nefarious part of this tragedy.

For these reasons, the invincible executive always comes clean and bounces back. It is simple advice that has saved many careers. And, even more important, as recent corporate scandals attest, the failure to heed this advice has cost hundreds of executives their livelihoods, and many their freedom.

Learn to Take a Punch

┌─ **📷 SNAPSHOT** ──────────────────────

Have you ever been falsely accused of improper or unethical
conduct?

Yes: 64 percent   **No:** 36 percent
└───

The French general and emperor Napoleon Bonaparte retreated
twice for every time he advanced. He did not have to win all the
time; he did not have to win most of the time; he had to win at *the
right time*. Napoleon's greatest skill was knowing *when not to fight*
and *when to cut his losses*. Let's discuss this issue in the modern corporate environment.

Earlier we discussed how invincible executives bounce back
from career setbacks. In this section we will deal with a particular
type of career problem that merits special attention: false or untrue
publicity. Almost two-thirds of invincible executives have had to
deal with untrue allegations about themselves or their companies,
and the means by which they deal with this situation provide significant insight into the way they manage their careers.

False or untrue publicity can be something as big as a story
about you in the *National Enquirer* or as small as a backstabbing

coworker. But the rules for dealing with false publicity are pretty much the same any way it comes at you.

One-Fifth Are for Fighting

Only about one in five invincible executives adopts a take-no-prisoners approach to false or untrue publicity. Tom Cruise, it seems, will sue anyone who publishes (seriously) false information about him. Former House Minority Leader Richard Gephardt also believes that, if you are confronted by untrue publicity, "you cannot let it hang out there. You have to deal with it immediately because people don't know the facts and they are impressed with the facts that they are given. You have to go right at the people putting out the untrue publicity and clear it up right away." Former Senator Alan Simpson agrees: "An attack unanswered is an attack believed," he stated. In the corporate world, Pat Finneran of Boeing said virtually the same thing—noting that he had been successful taking "head-on" untrue publicity about his company. So there is no doubt that many top professionals—ranging from movie stars to politicians to corporate leaders—will not tolerate untrue publicity. Nevertheless, while this approach can be promising, satisfying, and successful, it is the exception, not the rule.

The reason why many decide not to take on untrue publicity is simple. Slanderers very often find a way to get in the last word. Remember that once someone has abandoned the truth, that person has no constraints on what he or she can and will say about you. In the case of a backstabbing coworker, "Even if you get the coworker fired," a software CEO once told me, "they will start some sort of e-mail campaign, or in the worst cases, file a whistle-blower lawsuit against you." Often suits for harassment or unethical conduct are really the last-ditch tactics of disgruntled coworkers who will do anything to win a personality conflict.

And if a member of the media is the slanderer, of course, he or she has total control over how your viewpoints are expressed, if that person chooses to print your views at all. "The press always has the last word. They'll put a correction in under weather reports from Singapore," notes Marriott executive vice president Joe Ryan. Or as banker–baseball team owner Drew Baur put it, "You don't get into a fight with somebody who has more ink than you do." Fighting back might feel good at first, but often it either does no good or simply results in more mudslinging. Everyone gets dirty, and you might even call more attention to the falsehood by responding.

Two-Fifths Ignore

At the other extreme, about two in five invincible executives will generally ignore bad press. Ron Gafford of Austin Industries echoed the sentiments of many corporate leaders on the subject of untrue publicity when he said to me, "We elect the 'do nothing' strategy. Any request for retraction or clarification will probably only exacerbate the problem. We just let it die a natural death."

Sheryl Crow has a similar perspective. She believes that as soon as you get to the top of an industry or profession, there is likely to be a natural backlash against you. There will be jealous or resentful people, and there is not a lot you can do about it. Ms. Crow has concluded that negative publicity is part of the way the world of success works, and so what is the use in fighting it? She experienced such a backlash after the Grammy-winning success of her first record, *Tuesday Night Music Club*. While the single said "All I wanna do is have some fun," she found herself in a situation that was anything but that. The musicians who helped her with the record made accusations that she was not giving them enough credit, and a jealous disagreement arose. "So what happened was I became well known because it was my record, and a lot of other people felt that they should have become famous. And no matter how much press I did about the other people involved, the press was really only interested in me, the artist. So it was a really hard lesson because I lost the support of my friends." Crow chose not to engage in a public fight in the media with her former friends. "I just retreated," she told me. Ultimately, the incident had no negative effect on her career.

One reason to ignore bad publicity is that people only pay enough attention to it to believe that it is true. They rarely follow the details of the public debate. For example, a prominent broadcaster recently had to deal with a scandalous allegation about his personal life. A media outlet reported an untrue story that he was in a rehabilitation clinic for sexual addiction when he was actually risking his life in Israel covering the conflict between the Israelis and Palestinians. He too chose to ignore the bad publicity. He realized that by making an issue of it, he would call even further attention to the matter and probably increase the perception that the ridiculous story was true.

The Rest of Them Work the Soft Kill

So 20 percent fight the falsehoods, and 40 percent ignore it. From my interviews, it seems that if you are thick-skinned enough to ignore bad publicity, it will usually blow over. But not always. In some cases, ignoring the bad press or rumors could have lasting negative consequences. About 40 percent of invincible executives regularly conclude that it is worth investing time and energy to work a serious PR problem. When they or their organizations find themselves wrongfully accused of improper conduct, they set out to correct the falsehood in a tactful, but very tactical, manner. Here is the process that seems to work for them.

First, they have a standard by which they weed out the inconsequential falsehoods. They make this determination by analyzing the negative effect that the publicity is having on their careers and/or companies versus the cost of responding in terms of time, energy, and the risk of fanning the flames. Automobile executive Jack Schmitt told me that "if the falsehood is in the public eye, we ask if the information has a shelf life of more than two weeks— meaning that we ask, 'Will this blow over in two weeks or will it probably be worse?' " Joe Ryan of Marriott also believes that any rumor that has the momentum to build for two weeks is dangerous enough that he will work the problem. On the other hand, if the bad PR is an internal company issue, Ryan asks if it has a shelf life of more than *two days*. The internal "shelf life" period is shorter than the external one because adverse rumors inside a company have an immediate negative effect on productivity. Internal rumors are actually worse than bad press. If the answer to the shelf life question is yes, his company develops a plan to fix the problem.

Janet Reno probably knows more about dealing with bad publicity than anyone I interviewed for the book. Despite Waco, the Elian Gonzales controversy, "Saturday Night Live" skits, her chilly relationship with some Clinton administration officials, and a loss in the Florida governor's race, she remains a very popular figure among the majority of Americans—and she is particularly popular among women. How does she handle untrue publicity? First, she adopts a presumption that the person making the false statement has good intentions. Then she engages in a dialogue to try to correct the errors. If she learns that there are ulterior motives and there is no way she is going to get the truth out, then she ignores the bad publicity. But more often than not, she can engage in a constructive dialogue.

Coolheaded, constructive dialogue in the face of bad publicity is very difficult because the natural tendency is to launch a "nuclear" counteroffensive against the slanderers. After all, these people are spreading false information. Remember, however, most people who spread false information about you either (1) believe that the false information is true, or (2) believe that you have behaved so unethically that spreading lies about you is their only defense.

Ms. Reno also recognizes the incredible value of humor in defusing false publicity. Just after she left office, she went on "Saturday Night Live" and crashed the "Janet Reno's Disco Party" skit that the cast had been doing for years with one of the male cast members dressed up like her. It became a classic moment in TV and made her look great. In a similar vein, in 1984 President Reagan had to address serious questions about his mental capacity after a poor showing in his first debate with Democratic nominee and former Vice President Walter Mondale. He made the classic quip that age was not an issue because he was not "going to exploit, for political purposes, my opponent's youth and inexperience." That one line ended the issue of his competence and stopped the bad press in its tracks.

Hendrik Verfaillie, former CEO of Monsanto, agrees with Ms. Reno on the subject of untrue publicity. "The best way to handle it is with very open, transparent dialogue," he says. To illustrate the point, Mr. Verfaillie related this story to me. Prior to his becoming CEO, the management of Monsanto believed that genetically engineered food was the wave of the future—that by increasing yield through gene alteration, the problem of world hunger could be solved. They were committed to saving millions of lives with their new products. There was tremendous enthusiasm within the company for genetically engineered food. Monsanto believed that its commitment to reducing hunger would give it the reputation as the most responsible corporation in the world.

Much to the shock of Monsanto executives, widespread protests against genetically engineered food erupted in the late 1990s. Opponents of genetic engineering claimed that the food could cause medical problems for people who ate it, that it would contribute to disease, and that it would have catastrophic environmental effects.

Because, Monsanto officials believed, there was no credible scientific data to support these contentions, Monsanto's management underestimated the potential effect of these protests—choosing for the most part to ignore them or dismiss their importance. What happened? The protests gained momentum and the volume of bad publicity increased dramatically. A large portion of the world's population began to oppose genetically engineered grains—even though Monsanto executives believed that their better yields represented a great possibility in the war on starvation.

Once Monsanto realized the magnitude of the problem— around the time that Mr. Verfaillie became CEO—a group of executives wanted to launch a counteroffensive to get the truth out. Verfaillie, however, adopted a more refined approach. He refused to demonize those who were spreading false information about his company's products. "What we had done is really defend our position and take the position that the other guys were just not smart enough to get it. We were right; they were wrong. What we found was that you cannot get dialogue that way. . . . By a willingness to listen, however, and by being open to the arguments of the other side—and by accepting that we might not always have the full truth—we started getting a better dialogue. We listened to their position and now we have a real possibility of getting together."

Mr. Verfaillie sat down and met with the leaders of the groups that opposed genetically engineered food. Initially, he was in a listening mode. He was not there to convince them that they were wrong. He wanted to understand whether they really believed what they were saying. The first step in defusing the situation was self-education. He determined that most members of the opposition did in fact believe what they were saying. Much to his surprise, he found that they were sincere.

While this dialogue did not eliminate the problem, it brought the bad publicity almost totally under control. The minority of extremists who spread the lies were separated from the sincere people who wanted to know the truth, and the result has been a defusing of the problem and a sharp reduction in negative press.

This process of (1) meeting the other side, (2) listening to them, (3) determining whether they are acting in good faith, and (4), if they are in fact operating in good faith, engaging in dialogue, is a very common pattern among executives who enjoy prolonged success.

Subconscious Payback

Even more interestingly, you will often find that the person who made negative statements will bend over backward to do something nice for you later on. Admiral Joseph Prueher advocates developing a "media bank account." You make some "investments" by helping out media personnel from time to time with stories, and then when you need some help from the media, you can make a "withdrawal."

Southwest Airlines CEO Jim Parker told me an interesting story along these lines. He considers Southwest to be a "media-friendly company," and he personally likes reporters. However, he recalls one instance where a reporter for a major newspaper had run a story critical of Southwest's labor relations policies. Southwest's management felt that the article was unfair and communicated its concerns to the newspaper—but in an even-tempered, respectful, and private manner. A couple of weeks later, the same paper ran a very favorable feature story about the airline. Parker does not believe it was an accident. Rather, he believes that the careful cultivation of a good relationship with the media—even when you are disappointed with a particular story or commentary—almost always produces tangible positive results in the future.

I call this phenomenon the "subconscious payback"—and it is a common theme among people who deal with publicity issues successfully. Even the sports world lends support to this idea. Former

Chicago Blackhawks center Adam Creighton discussed with me the subconscious payback phenomenon in professional hockey when dealing with referees and linesmen. "If the referee makes a bad call, and you let him know it in a respectful rather than angry way, more often than not, a judgment call will go your way later in the game. It's not something intentional on the part of the ref, it's just human nature," he says.

The same principles hold true for smaller-scale PR nightmares, such as the actions of backstabbing coworkers. More often than not, you can totally disarm backstabbers by getting to know them, showing respect for their viewpoints, and then slowly trying to bring them around. The person might not apologize or correct past wrongdoings, but you will find that he or she will stand up for you in the most unlikely circumstances down the road.

Legal Intervention

There may well be a time, however, in your career when you are dealing with a person who is genuinely dishonest and out to get you. There is no chance at all that reason and sincerity will placate the liar—be it a member of the media, a competitor, or someone within your organization. It is in these situations that invincible executives realize that they need professional help. Many people make career-ending mistakes at the time when they are receiving some bad PR. They write angry or aggressive e-mails that get into the wrong hands. They lose their cool in front of a camera. They fire someone without properly documenting the reasons. They self-destruct.

When confronted with seriously false allegations that could jeopardize your company or career, the best thing you can do is get a skilled lawyer and professional media adviser into the picture early. The reason for getting the lawyer transcends good advice.

Communications made to or from a lawyer during a dispute, or even communications between nonlawyers made at the direction of a lawyer, are usually protected from disclosure to any third party by the attorney-client privilege. This privilege is a secret weapon that the vast majority of top executives use—even though many will not admit it. The privilege effectively immunizes you from the effects of your own misstatements or emotional outbursts. According to Pat Finneran of Boeing, most good executives have a special relationship with a lawyer or two, whom they use strategically as sounding boards to get them out of nasty situations, but whom they also use tactically to get a cloak of protection around their communications. The lawyer then helps that person decide—in a reasoned, protected environment—how to proceed against the individual or organization who is making the false allegations.

Behind every invincible executive, there are a couple of trusted lawyers and similar such advisers. While I, as a lawyer by trade, may have a conflict of interest in saying so, I firmly believe that the executives who hate the lawyers are the ones who go down in flames—and I can give you a lot of examples to support the point. Keep in mind that valuing legal advice is very different from valuing lawsuits. The best lawyers keep you out of court 98 percent of the time. So swallow hard, and take the advice. Get to know a good attorney, and make him or her a friend, make him or her part of your inner circle. It is a like buying career insurance.

Work Is a Member of the Family

📷 **SNAPSHOT**

Have you been able to balance professional goals with personal and family goals?

Yes: 42 percent   **No:** 58 percent

I asked a lot of top professionals whether they are good at balancing their work activities with their family and outside interests. Barrett A. Toan, CEO of the multibillion-dollar pharmacy software company Express Scripts, gave me a succinct answer that echoed the sentiments of many others: "Not particularly."

A startling number of the invincible executives I have known are single or have divorced. About 15 percent have spouses who live or work in a different city than they do; and these executives catch up with their families on weekends, holidays, and vacations. Those who have remained married for a long time usually have stay-at-home spouses who have decided that supporting their spouse's career is their career. Because traditions erode slowly and top executives tend to be in their fifties or sixties, the stay-at-home spouses tend to be the wives. However, that trend is changing as well. In my own experience, a friend of mine recently quit his law practice to stay at home with the kids because his wife's medical practice was taking off in a big way. In fact, homemaker husbands now run approximately one in six households.

Career as a Top Priority

Because the invincible executive needs to be mobile, his family tends to move with him early in his career. However, at some point, the family (most often the stay-at-home spouse) may decide that the interests of the kids require more stability. As a result, the further an invincible executive is into his or her career, the more likely it is that his or her family will live in a different city. "There came a time when the kids and I said, 'We are not moving again. Our schools are here, our friends are here, and we love our house,'" the wife of a top executive at Johnson & Johnson told me recently. This may not sound like encouraging news for young people who aspire to great professional success.

But you know something? Most top executives accept the difficult balance between job and family without questioning it. Those who have experienced dizzying professional triumph do not do much hand-wringing about the state of their family lives. Yes, they wish that their first marriage had held up. Yes, they hate commuting to a different city. *But they have made a commitment to achieve career success and everyone else is going to have to get used to it or get out of their lives.*

"I treat my job like another member of the family," a young, ambitious pharmaceutical executive told me on an airplane a few months ago. "It gets the same attention, time, and nurturing as anyone else, and just like inter-sibling jealousy, if you're jealous of my career, *get over it!*" Similarly, Tom O'Neill, CEO of Parsons Brinckerhoff, told me, "I sort of gave up on the idea of achieving a very harmonious balance between work and home."

Unfortunately, however, a large percentage—almost half—of invincible executives have expressed some regrets about their relationships with their children. Several of the country's most well-known executives and politicians confided to me that they have had very difficult periods as parents. Combine two simple facts and it should be no surprise that family harmony can suffer when the father or mother is a professional star: First, the child of an invincible executive almost by definition feels tremendous pressure to succeed like his or her father or mother did. Most children in this situation simply will not enjoy the same levels of success. Then, throw in the fact that the parent was gone a lot when the child was young, and it becomes easy for the child to blame his or her failure to live up to the parent's success on the lack of parental presence. This is a recurrent theme among top professionals.

This book is not about the invincible father, or the invincible wife. So you are going to have to make a decision. Two of the brightest lawyers I have ever met decided at a midpoint in their careers that they were not ever going to consider their jobs to be anywhere near as important as their families. That is a noble and admirable decision. They took themselves off the stellar career trajectories. But if you want to get to the top, you have to put the job right up there with the family—not higher, but on almost the same plane. Obviously, a family emergency trumps everything, but short of that, there will be many times when the career wins out over the family.

Expanding Family Time

The good news is that most invincible executives eventually iron out their problems with their children, and many enjoy happy marriages as well, although often it is the second marriage that proves to be the lasting one.

Now there are a couple of tricks to making the family situation work. I got these pointers principally from two men who have enjoyed good family lives throughout their careers despite a lot of mobility and time away from their families—Mike Sears, the executive vice president and CFO of Boeing, and Admiral Joseph Prueher, former commander of the Pacific Fleet and U.S. ambassador to China.

First, learn to operate on less sleep. Sears needs only three hours per night. Military people like Admiral Prueher tend to become accustomed to low amounts of sleep as well. A surprising number of invincible executives throughout history—including, for example, Albert Einstein—have noted how much more you can get done if you are awake three more hours each day—that's 12.5 percent of a day, which gives you a real advantage over those who need a lot of sleep!

While I am no doctor and cannot comment on the medical aspects of the debate, there is no doubt that invincible executives believe that reducing your sleep time is something you can learn. They point out, for example, that part of the essential training of interns and residents at hospitals involves lowering your threshold of sleep so that you can operate effectively on two or three hours of sleep and feel well-rested on five hours. Catnaps—fifteen-minute interludes of sleep during the day—are another surprisingly common scenario among top executives. If you can learn to operate on less sleep, you will get your work done faster and have more flexibility to spend time with your family.

Vigorous regular exercise and maintaining a proportionate height-to-weight ratio will help you reduce your need for sleep. After that, it is just a question of setting the alarm earlier and going to bed later! I did it so that I can write and practice law at the same time, and I guarantee you it works.

Now a lot of people out there will object strongly to this strategy. They write books and go on "Oprah" saying that Americans need more sleep, and there have been studies suggesting that everyone needs seven or eight hours of sleep. You may like this idea. That's fine, but it may mean that you are not the invincible executive. Like it or not, executives with staying power tend to function on less sleep than other people do.

Second, invincible executives, while passionate about their careers, are able to "carve out" family time. They have an amazing ability *not to take work home with them—either physically or psychologically*. When they are at home, most of them do not prepare for meetings, write memos, or even use their work cell phones—except in the most extreme or unusual circumstances. Few of them wake up at night worried about a precarious deal falling through or the latest earnings projections. They would rather stay at the office late or even over a weekend than mingle their home lives with their work lives. Careful segregation of family time—even if it is less time than most people devote to their families—goes a long way toward keeping the family of an invincible executive cohesive and happy.

If you want to become an invincible executive, you are going to have to throw out a few preconceptions and clichés. You and your family will need to agree that the career is part of the family. You may have to be careful in setting expectations for your children. You may have to get accustomed to the idea that you will not live in the same city as your family for extended periods of time. You might learn to get by on less sleep. You should turn your cell phone off when you are at home. And you should not feel bad about any of it.

Find a Job That You Look Forward to Every Day

> 📷 **SNAPSHOT**
>
> Do you have any regrets about the work you chose to do?
> **Yes:** 0 percent   **No:** 100 percent

Surveys, while varied, show that up to 90 percent of Americans do not like their jobs. Many people who are very good at their jobs do not like what they do. What about people who have reached the very top? We know that invincible executives do not feel guilty about making their jobs a big part of their lives, but do they really like what they do?

The universal consensus is yes—they love their jobs passionately. As manufacturing guru Sam Fox puts it, "I hate the phrase TGI Friday. It denotes displeasure with one's job. I prefer TGI Monday. I can't wait to get back to work!" Richard Bell, chairman and CEO of HDR, Inc., feels the same way. "I literally want to run to work every day," he says. Bill Winter, chairman emeritus of Dr. Pepper/Seven Up, Inc., said to me, "There was never a morning when I got up and said I would rather stay at home than go to the office." Consistently, Juanita Hinshaw, CFO of Graybar Electric, considers liking what you do to be at the top of the list of the most important factors in achieving long-term success—and she has advised many people of the importance of picking a profession that you are not only good at, but that you enjoy in every respect.

On the flip side, one of the surest ways to failure is to enter a profession that you do not like. "You can be successful for years at something you do not like, but eventually you will become so angry or careless that you will make a big mistake," a prominent Midwestern attorney once said to me. Leading medical researcher Joshua Korzenik agrees: "You are not going to reach your whole potential unless you really like what you are doing. . . . You can be good and make money, but you are not going to get to the next level. One of the things that is absolutely critical to getting to the top is that you have got to love what you are doing." Moreover, according to Congressman Gephardt, even if you start out liking what you do, "you cannot lose interest" or people will notice, and your career will suffer immediate negative effects.

Similarly, when I asked former Senator Bob Dole the major flaws that cause talented people to fail, he listed "taking advantage of power" as number one, but as a close second, he said "getting into something that you do not believe in." As an example, Senator Dole pointed out what happened to President Johnson after he became embroiled in the Vietnam War in the 1960s. President Johnson, a man who had coveted the presidency for decades and finally achieved his goal, found himself deeply embroiled in an unpopular war that he did not truly support. Yet the nation was too committed at that point just to withdraw, or so President Johnson believed. This terrible situation demoralized the president so badly that he decided not to run for reelection and retired from politics.

Find Your Passion—Among the Things You're Good At

While earlier in the book we discussed the need to find your talents, we did not discuss the need to find your passion. And there is a reason why I saved the part about finding your passion for the end of the career path section of the book: because everyone says "find your passion" as if that's all you need to become a great success. I did not want the passion part to overshadow the more nuts-and-bolts aspects of the invincible career path, so I saved it for the end of this part of the book.

So, yes, you have to find something you really like, but finding that passion must be put in the context of everything else that you need to do to become the invincible executive. Passion alone gets you nothing. You need to acknowledge at the outset that just because you are passionate about a career or skill does not mean you are good at it. In fact, it is better to be talented and hate your job than to lack talent and like it. There are a lot of people who get pretty far in the world doing something that they absolutely despise. There are very few people who get far in a field they love but for which they lack ability.

However, every invincible executive I interviewed—dozens of them—said that you will never get to the very top of a profession that you do not like. "You can get pretty far," an air force general told me, "but you'll never get the star." The upper echelon requires both talent and passion.

There are skills that you have that you do not like using. I know, for example, many people who are good at math but do not like it. A couple of them were so good that they allowed teachers, parents, and bosses to commandeer their careers—pushing them into engineering and software design. One of them had tears well up in his eyes when he confided to me that he knew he would be the best literature professor in the world, but instead he is designing hydraulics systems for cars. You cannot become this person.

Find what you are good at; then, only within that skill set, do what you like.

The Chains of Money

My mentor, Senator John Danforth, told me at lunch a few months back, "When it is all over and you are retired, you have to be able to look back at your life and not feel like you wasted it. And if that means that you switch careers, do it. If that means less money, do it."

The invincible executive "does not define success by a title," according to Express Scripts CEO Barrett Toan. The key to success is intellectual satisfaction, according to Toan. Congressman Gephardt agrees: "The main thing is to be intellectually stimulated and interested in what you are doing," he notes. Money is not the primary motivator either. Most top professionals are well-off, but they do not equate financial success with professional success— and few of them started out with expectations of riches. Manufacturing giant Sam Fox's motto is: "Don't show me the money. When you are looking for a job, do not look for the job that pays the most. Look for the job that fits your particular skills and that which you are going to enjoy."

For example, Dr. Joshua Korzenik is one of the nation's leading researchers in the area of gastrointestinal disorders. He is an invincible executive in the field of medical research—with a stellar worldwide reputation. He has often thought of how much more money he could be making in private practice. While he does fine financially, he knows he is helping more people by forgoing the big bucks and devoting his talents to medical research. Instead of making money, he is making a difference, he told me with great sincerity. He loves the "sense of service" his job gives him.

An acquaintance of mine who was a young partner in a super-prestigious law firm recently left the firm to become an adviser to the Bush administration on immigration policy. He left his law practice right at the time when his compensation would have increased exponentially—into the high six figures. Now he is working on our country's post-9/11 immigration policy for a fraction of the money that he could have made in private practice. However, he knows that the fruit of his labor will likely influence the future of our country. When I had dinner with him last spring, I asked him if he had any regrets leaving all that money behind. "Tom," he said, "I am having a blast."

In addition, he is young enough that there is still time to make money later on. It is amazing how easy it is to make money if you can distinguish yourself in a field *without regard to the money*. Low-paid politicians become highly paid lobbyists—if they ultimately decide they need the cash. Low-paid military officers who distinguish themselves become highly paid executives and consultants later on. Do what you love and what you are good at without regard to money, and the odds are that the money will follow.

THE INVINCIBLE PERSONALITY

Now it is time to move from the external career paths of invincible executives to their inner workings. In Part II, we will go into the minds of invincible executives to explore their emotional and spiritual makeup. We will answer such questions as, What role do anger and fear play in the personality of a person who makes it to the top? How do top professionals size up other people when deciding whether to work with them? What role do loyalty, friendship, and spirituality play in their professional lives?

There is less unanimity among top professionals about what personality characteristics lead to success than there was on the subject of career planning that we discussed in Part I. However, once we scratch the surface, it will become clear that most of the differences in the viewpoints among the interviewees are the result of a distinct evolution over the past twenty-five years in the personality qualities that lead to success. What worked twenty-five years ago does not work today. Consequently, more senior invincible executives tend to have one set of personality characteristics, while younger ones value and display a slightly different set of characteristics. Let's study the personalities of executives with staying power.

11

Anger Is a Tactic,
Not an Emotion

┌─ 📷 **SNAPSHOT** ─────────────────────────────────┐

What role do anger and temper play in your professional
personality?

Major: 28 percent **Minor:** 72 percent
└───┘

Adam, the popular and visionary CEO of a major automotive supply company in the deep South, arrived at his company's headquarters one morning around 8:45 A.M. When he walked in the
building, he noticed that cubicle after cubicle and office after office
were empty. Adam had a strong work ethic and believed his
employees should get in the same time he did. When he saw the
empty offices, he began to doubt his employees shared his beliefs.
So he wrote his employees—all eight thousand of them—an angry
e-mail telling them that they had better shape up or he would mete
out all kinds of punishment. One of the employees decided to post
the e-mail on an Internet chat line. The investing public got the
e-mail and immediately started selling the stock, fearing that the
company was not productive. The stock lost 20 percent of its value

in one day. Although Adam's company recovered under his strong leadership, Adam learned a lesson about the possible unintended consequences of angry e-mail.

Joe, a mid-level program manager at a major aerospace company, also let his anger get the best of him. He managed a program that built actuator assemblies for commercial aircraft. The program had a lot of problems, which Joe blamed on the customer, who constantly changed the design of the actuators. The customer blamed Joe and his company for building allegedly defective actuators. Eventually the customer terminated Joe's company for default and sued his company for about a million dollars, claiming breach of the actuator contract. The million dollars represented the marginal or "delta" cost of getting a new company in quickly to build the actuators—in other words, the new company charged a million more than Joe's did.

Then something even worse happened. In the lawsuit, the customer subpoenaed all of Joe's documents, including his personal notes, day planners, and e-mails. Those notes, planners, and e-mails had numerous profane remarks about the customer, including such gems as:

"If those SOB's don't stop jerking my chain, I am going to slow down the work on the project and watch them f***ers wither out and dry when their customer gets mad!! Without my actuators, they can't build their planes. They can eat s***!"

I put the one e-mail in this book so you can get an idea of just how bad the situation was. Add seventeen or so more statements just like it, and you get the whole picture.

As soon as the customer's lawyers got these documents, they amended their lawsuit against Joe and his company to ask for punitive damages. They claimed that the profane e-mails were evidence of malicious intent, entitling them to big money. In fact, the customer asked for $15 million in damages for tortious interference with contract—all over and above the initial $1 million that the customer sought for the alleged breach of contract. What had been a manageable $1 million problem was now a $16 million problem spinning out of control.

Joe claimed he was just blowing off some steam and never thought the notes and e-mails would see the light of day. Unfortunately, as a result of the increased potential liability for the company, Joe's CEO got involved and settled the case out of court for over $5 million. Joe had spent twenty-two years at the company and had stellar performance reviews, but the only thing the CEO knew about him was that he had written a slew of profane notes and e-mails about a customer that cost the company $5 million. That was the end of Joe's career in program management.

Don't Lose Your Cool

"Lose your temper and you have lost the game," says Sam Fox of the Harbour Group. In an era when e-mails and the Internet can spread news to anyone and everyone immediately, where voice mails are provided no legal privacy protection, and where business-by-subpoena has become business as usual, you can be sure that any time you let your emotion get the better of your reason, you are no longer invincible. Someone who does not have your best interests at heart will use your outburst against you. The era when you can fly off the handle on a regular basis is officially over. For that reason, the vast majority of invincible executives under the age of fifty say that they make minimal use of anger in the workplace. Many of those over fifty, like Stephen Lambright of Anheuser-Busch, have changed with the times, acknowledging that they have "mellowed" over the past several years. Lambright says he used to get mad a lot; now he has evolved to a point that he controls his temper much better than he once did.

Doug Bain of Boeing uses the "safety valve" approach to professional anger. When something incenses you at the workplace, first you "spout off to someone you trust," then you "calm down and determine if there is anything you can do about it." If so, you take reasoned action. Dave Ruf, CEO of Burns & McDonnell, puts a time limit on his anger: "You have the right to get upset for ten minutes," says Ruf—and then it is on to more productive pursuits.

Some organizations consciously cultivate a culture that dampens anger in the workplace. Earl Graves, the publisher of *Black Enterprise* magazine, started his career as an assistant to Robert F. Kennedy. He recalls Senator Kennedy had an absolute rule in his office: You do not blow up at people. Period. Some corporations also foster a "no anger" culture quite consciously. For example, I interviewed the CEO, president, and executive vice president of Marriott International for this book. Although the three interviews were separate, Messrs. Marriott, Shaw, and Ryan all said virtually the same thing about anger in the workplace: that Marriott fosters a culture that rejects incivility and public outbursts. As Bill Marriott put it, "There is a time when you can show displeasure, and you should show it only with the people who might have done something that you're not pleased with. I think doing it in a public forum or a large group of people, you just can't do it." Similarly, Marriott's president, Bill Shaw, said, "I think it is important that you are predictable, as far as your behavior, and people find it difficult to . . . get behind a leader who is volatile and would have temper tantrums." Echoing the same sentiment, Marriott executive vice president Joe Ryan said, "To me, it is very hard to build a genuine team when anger and temper are all part of it."

A Special Note for Women

Juanita Hinshaw, CFO of the multibillion-dollar technology company Graybar Electric, gives a particular admonition against anger, temper, and aggression to women executives. She believes that many women try to imitate men and their testosterone levels in business. They "try to be men, imitating male mentors" and consequently "become overly aggressive in their business dealings." Hinshaw considers such an approach to be a big career mistake. "While women should be assertive, they cannot be as overtly aggressive as men," she claims. Consequently, women should use anger very "sparingly" or they will become resented, hated, and completely ineffective on the job. It is not fair that this rule applies even more to women than men, perhaps, but it is reality.

The Dustup

However, while most top professionals use anger sparingly, few invincible executives of any age try to suppress their anger entirely. "Anger is a tactic, not an emotion," a two-star army special operations general told me several months back. In the military, there is no doubt that your sergeant or commanding officer is going to yell and scream at you. But you know from the beginning that the person is not really mad at you—rather it is a tactic to promote discipline. As contradictory as it sounds, there is a way to distill the emotion out of the anger, leaving just the anger to be used in an appropriate, controlled manner.

Jim Parker, CEO of Southwest Airlines, agrees. "Sometimes you need to use anger to deliver a message forcefully." He adds, however, that "you can only display anger after you have had a chance to do some serious intellectual reflection." You cannot fly off the handle and lose control. Rather, you have to decide that anger is the appropriate tactic in a given situation.

Former senator and presidential candidate Bob Dole notes that some of his colleagues in the United States Senate had fiery tempers, but again, they did not lose control when they were unhappy with an opponent or colleague. According to Dole, they had a motto: "Use your temper, don't lose your temper." Good politicians consider loss of temper to be a valuable tactic in carefully planned situations. Former prosecutor and prominent Democrat Ed Dowd makes the same point when he says, "You cannot let your anger use you."

For example, former Senator, Special Counsel, and diplomat John Danforth is an Episcopal priest known for his calm and respectful demeanor. Many of his staffers say they have *never* seen him get mad. But even he will tell you that sometimes it is necessary to have a "dustup"—as he calls it—in order to achieve a particular and specific political end.

For example, when Attorney General Reno appointed Danforth Special Counsel to investigate the Waco tragedy, he had to contend with a parallel congressional investigation led by fellow Republican Senator Arlen Specter. Danforth did not believe that parallel investigations would be productive. He discussed the matter with Senator Specter and thought he had secured an agreement with his fellow Republicans that the congressional investigation would stop. However, Danforth soon learned that one of Senator Specter's investigators was at Waco interviewing people.

Danforth called his staff in and said with a smile, "It's time for a little dustup." He instructed one staffer to draft a righteously indignant letter to Senator Specter and copy the letter to the Democrats on the Senate Judiciary Committee. The letter was curt and to the point, but not aggressive. At Danforth's direction, the letter used none of the adjectives such as "outrageous" or "ludicrous" that tend to characterize angry correspondence and, obviously, the letter contained no profanity. But the anger was clear simply from its succinct exposition of the facts—a promise made and a promise broken.

Danforth then instructed another staff member to call all the key witnesses in Waco and direct them not to speak with the congressional investigators—even if it put Danforth in contempt of Congress for interfering with a congressional inquiry. "Let them haul the Special Counsel into Congress on contempt charges," he said. "That would be great." He knew they would never do it.

Needless to say, Danforth's letter was made public by the Democrats, and the witnesses who had been told not to cooperate with Congress also made public statements to that effect as well. The Republicans on the Judiciary Committee were outraged and made all kinds of emotional, threatening statements to the media and elsewhere that stood in marked contrast to Senator Danforth's more controlled use of anger. And guess what happened? After a meeting, the Republicans who controlled the Judiciary Committee wrote Senator Danforth a letter agreeing to stop their investigation.

Danforth's tactical use of anger worked for several reasons that characterize the personality of the invincible executive. First, Danforth used anger sparingly. He had developed the reputation as a peaceful Episcopal priest, so when he did get angry, people took note. Second, he never exhibited emotion in a public forum. He did not write nasty e-mails, leave aggressive voice mails, or go in front of the camera ranting and raving. Rather, he tactically placed a very businesslike letter such that he looked like he was the reasonable one. Third, he let others—the Democrats and the witnesses—get his message out. He never made any public statement that could be cut and pasted or distorted by someone who did not have his well-being at heart. He had mastered the art of the tactical use of anger.

Anger in Style

The above stories—showing both inappropriate and appropriate uses of anger at work—make four basic points: (1) uncontrolled emotion disrupts the workplace and alienates employees; (2) employees have ways of getting back at bosses who berate them—

ranging from whistleblower lawsuits to the Internet; (3) there is no place for profanity or similarly aggressive choices of words in recorded professional communications (*recorded* meaning e-mail, voice mail, interviews, meetings where minutes are taken, legal proceedings, letters, videotaped statements, etc.); and (4), despite all that, the well-considered, occasional, and purely tactical use of anger can pay off in a big way.

There are two other points about the use of anger that came out of my interviews and experiences with invincible executives. First, you need an *anger style*. Ranting and raving does not cut it anymore. For example, Janet Reno said that when she is angry at someone, "I lower my voice and I get more steady in my tone of voice." One of her former staffers confirmed to me that it is both intimidating and totally unnerving to have to stretch to hear her when she is mad. Everyone knows that "when she whispers, someone screwed up big time." She has developed a very effective anger style.

Former Wyoming Senator Alan Simpson told me, "There is a way to tell a guy to go to hell in a way that he actually looks forward to the trip." You can get mad in a way that the person who is the subject of the anger actually thanks you for bringing the issue to his or her attention. A calm, firm tone of voice, combined with a well-organized exposition of the facts that got you mad, usually achieves the desired result.

Similarly, a federal judge told me in chambers one day that you know when he is mad because he "starts the sarcasm." He always mixes a dry, sarcastic humor in with his anger in order to defuse the situation. I once observed him tell an attorney that he did not want to hear oral argument on a particular motion because the point of law at issue had already been decided against that attorney. The attorney noticed up a hearing on the motion anyway. When the lawyer began to argue why the judge should grant the motion, the judge listened quietly for about thirty seconds. Then, out of the blue, the judge yelled the letter "D!" as loud as he could. The attorney arguing the motion, along with everyone else in the courtroom, stopped in his tracks. No one knew why the judge had just yelled out the letter "D." The judge smiled, but he said nothing else. After a few seconds of silence, the attorney resumed his passionate oral argument. Ten seconds passed and the judge yelled out the letter "E!" Silence again for a few seconds. The lawyer resumed his argument. About ten seconds later, the judge yelled out "N-I-E-D! Denied!" The whole courtroom cracked up hysterically. The judge looked at the lawyer, and said with a grin, "I told you not to raise that issue in my courtroom again. Next case." The gavel went down. Bang! There is an anger style.

Anger Parameters

The picture is getting clearer. Keep anger to a minimum. Make it a tactic rather than an emotion. Avoid profanity and public displays of anger. Develop an anger "style" that separates you from the ranters and ravers. And, finally, put outer parameters on your anger.

For example, never use anger arbitrarily. There are some well-known people who have gotten to the top of the heap by behaving so arbitrarily that people are scared to mess with them. History is in fact replete with them. It goes *way* back. For example, the Roman emperor Caligula had people executed almost at random. During the French Revolution, the Jacobins used the guillotine as an arbitrary weapon of terror. Joseph Stalin imposed order on the Soviet state in exactly that manner—the arbitrary exercise of power—purging even people loyal to him. These men got to the tops of their fields, right? Let's see now: Caligula was murdered. So were all of the Jacobin leaders. Stalin has gone down in history as the second worst leader ever, right behind Hitler—the true master of arbitrary anger.

Arbitrary action never wins in the long run—not for tyrants and dictators and not for modern-day executives. A few years ago, the business community was buzzing about the CEO of a major division of an aerospace company who was ousted by the board of directors while he was on a business trip to Europe. Stories emerged of the ousted CEO having called vice presidents into his office and berating or even firing them without notice. "He was the most arbitrary man I have ever encountered," one of his subordinates told me. "Eventually it caught up with him."

That is the final lesson about anger in the workplace: when you are angry, make sure that everyone understands why you are angry. While anger can be an effective professional tactic, anger devoid of reason never succeeds over the long haul.

Harness Your Fear
to Sharpen Your
Professional Judgment

📷 **SNAPSHOT**

Do you experience professional fear?

Yes: 80 percent   **No:** 20 percent

Many supposed experts, from the gung ho success gurus to elite advertising executives, preach that success requires "No Fear." On the surface, that slogan would seem to have some appeal. Certainly, many people are paralyzed into inaction or retreat by their fears. So how do invincible executives deal with fear? Do they experience it at all?

Macho Man and Superwoman?

I expected most of the executives I interviewed to say that they feel little or no fear in the workplace. After all, these people made it to the top, so they should have nothing to fear. Instead, I found that four out of five invincible executives acknowledge significant fear in performing their jobs. Interestingly, the women I interviewed tended to say that fear was counterproductive, and that they tried to suppress it wherever possible. The men, while by no means unanimous, most often said that they "used" fear to sharpen their skills. I attribute the difference between men and women in this regard to a greater concern by women that they will look weak if they show any fear. It is still tougher for a woman to get to the top, so fear suppression is a survival skill for many women.

Fear of Failure

Executives with staying power do not fear specific events or outcomes. Their fears are as unfocused as their career plans. In fact, when I asked top professionals what they feared, the phrase that I heard over and over in my interviews was a generalized "fear of failure." Senator Bob Dole used that phrase, as did Doug Bain of Boeing, Bruno Schmitter of Hydromat, and former U.S. Attorney Ed Dowd—who fears "failure in the courtroom" at every trial. Dave Ruf, the outgoing and hard-charging CEO of Burns & McDonnell, told me that, in order to be an effective CEO, "you have to run scared all of the time."

Hendrik Verfaillie, former CEO of Monsanto, summed it up this way: "One of the biggest drivers for many successful professionals is the fear of failure. And it's not so much the fear of the consequences—just the fear of failure. You want to be successful, and not being successful is almost unthinkable. It scares the hell out of me." Similarly, Barrett Toan, CEO of Express Scripts, said that "the fear of failure is probably the prime motivator for me. I think it is true for more people than you might think. You take a risk . . . and you're really motivated to succeed, not for the glory of the success but for the relief of not failing." Tom O'Neill of Parsons Brinckerhoff echoed these sentiments when he told me, "If we're all honest with each other, there is a fear of failure."

Fear of scandal is also a big motivator these days. Top executives look at what happened to the CEOs and top managers of Enron, ImClone, Tyco International, Arthur Andersen, ADM, Columbia HCA—even the battle that Carly Fiorina had with Walter Hewlett over the merger with Compaq—and they realize that, despite their competence and intelligence, (1) their careers are at the mercy of those who work for them, (2) their careers could be torpedoed immediately by one unhappy customer or ruthless competitor, and (3) their careers are one lightening-bolt scandal from being over. If a company does badly financially, or worse yet, finds itself the target of a whistleblower and/or criminal investigation (insider trading, antitrust violations, toxic waste dumping, accounting irregularities—there are so many possibilities), it is the senior manager who takes the blame, even if he or she was not directly involved in the factual scenario that led to the scandal.

"The shareholders hold the CEO responsible for everything that goes on in the company. If I knew about it, it is my fault. If I did not know about it, I should have. In that sense, the CEO has less control over his career than anyone else in the company," the CEO of a software company told me during a criminal investigation several years back.

Recently I defended a major manufacturing corporation in a high-profile criminal investigation. The news of the scandal had already been the subject of a "60 Minutes" segment. I met with a senior executive and several of his staff members to discuss the status of the matter. The senior executive had no involvement in the scandal other than being the fifth-level supervisor over the people who had allegedly committed the criminal acts—i.e., there were four supervisors between him and the alleged culprits. The executive had never even met the people who were being accused of the crime. At the end of the meeting, as everyone was leaving, he asked me to stay a minute. When everyone else was gone, this man—a gung ho ex-marine and Vietnam veteran—put his hand around my shoulder and softly said: "Tom, please don't let my family be publicly embarrassed. I have worked too hard to get here. I don't want to leave in shame."

What I saw was *the fear of failure dominating the mind of a decorated war hero.* Fortunately, the government dropped the investigation of the company after a few months, and this ex-marine went on to retire with his pride intact. But I saw how totally the fear of failure can dominate the minds of strong people. That means you should not fear fear itself.

Harnessing the Fear

Stephen Lambright, group vice president and general counsel of Anheuser-Busch, is a big, tough, confident man. But, like so many other top executives, he acknowledges that fear is part of his professional life and he is not ashamed to admit it. However, he notes, there is a big difference between fear and panic. "I think that a certain element of fear—as opposed to panic—is pretty darn healthy. It is like going into battle or going into a football game. You are a better player if you have a certain degree of fear. Some fear is healthy. But use it as a personal motivator rather than making it the message to everyone around you." Lieutenant General John Sams, former commander of the Fifteenth Air Force, said virtually the same thing: fear can sharpen you, but not if you let it paralyze you.

Indeed, a majority of invincible executives say that they can use their fear of failure to achieve positive results. A client who was in a real bind once told me, "Professional fear is like the first time you wear prescription sunglasses. You see everything in a darker shade, but with a sharpness and clarity that kind of jumps out at you."

Fear of failure sharpens the senses. Indeed, Lieutenant General Sams notes, "There is fear but it is not paralyzing fear. In fact, I tend to get better at what I am doing when there is fear in the picture because things tend to slow down for me when the pressure is on. I can see things more clearly and I'm able to react in a way that gives me greater vision into what is going on around me when things are totally in chaos. Things slow down and you are able to see better. . . . Fear *has to sharpen you* or you will be to some extent paralyzed by it."

Indeed, it is fear that causes invincible executives to take steps to reduce their risk of a career-ending scandal. These steps fall into four categories. First, the fear of failure allows invincible executives to focus their management efforts on obtaining a high-volume, unjaded information flow from their subordinates. Invincible executives create an environment, according to Mike Sears of Boeing, where people understand that they can and must flow problems in the company up the chain of command without concern that senior management will kill the messenger. Important news—be it good or bad—must get to senior management, and it is the responsibility of senior management to set up reporting structures that will allow information to get to them.

Invincible executives do not become insular. They do not isolate themselves by relying solely upon a small core of close friends and advisers. Instead, they keep lines of communication open between themselves and people two or three tiers below themselves in the organization. We will discuss this issue in depth in Part III.

Second, as I mentioned briefly before, invincible executives have to be willing to listen to the advice of the specialists—accountants, lawyers, environmental engineers, and media specialists. The CEOs who shun professional advice ("I hate those lawyers"; "Screw the accountants") are playing roulette with their careers. It is very common to hear senior executives speak disdainfully about lawyers, accountants, and other professional consultants. Those who really mean it often take a hard fall. More often than not, however, top executives place quiet reliance upon value-added specialists, and then tell the lawyer jokes for cover. "I think it is just a bunch of grandstanding when I hear top executives say that they do not need the lawyers and accountants. The really good ones rely heavily upon expertise," says Joe Durant, CEO of Westar Corporation. "If they do not, they get what is coming to them."

Adam Clymer, Washington correspondent for the *New York Times*, told me an interesting story about the failure to heed professional advice. Clymer told me that one of the flaws that led to the downfall of former House Speaker Newt Gingrich was that Gingrich often did not heed good advice of trained professionals. For example, Clymer told me about the time Gingrich and President Clinton were on Air Force One going to a funeral. Gingrich had hoped to spend some time with the president discussing budget issues during the trip but was not granted an audience with the president. Then, apparently Gingrich had to exit from the rear door of the plane. Gingrich was mad about the whole episode and wanted to comment publicly on it, but his press secretary told him not to say anything to anyone about the incident. Yet—against the advice of his press expert—Gingrich complained to the media about his treatment. It backfired. Gingrich was skewered by the press for acting like a big baby. There were even cartoons showing Gingrich in diapers crying. Clymer told me that Gingrich later confided to him that he should have listened to the experts but "he just couldn't help himself." Clymer added that Gingrich, though a brilliant man "bubbling with ideas," made this kind of mistake "again and again." "The unwillingness to pay attention to cautionary advice from staff" is a common theme in the downfall of politicians, according to Clymer.

Third, top executives obviously have to pick advisers they can trust. However, they often do not define trust with a broad enough brush. Trust encompasses not only morality, honesty, and loyalty, but also competence. Many flawed executives surround themselves with sycophants—friends or relatives who may be as honest and well-intentioned as they can be, but who are of such minimal competence that they simply defer to the boss on all issues. Being surrounded by weakness can give an executive a feeling of power and invincibility, but that feeling is a mirage. I have run into dozens of lame, untalented hangers-on in my career—consultants who flatter rather than analyze, lawyers who protect their careers before they protect the company, accountants who exercise no independent judgment whatsoever. I can spot them a mile away, and their incompetence almost always catches up with the people they are advising. True invincible executives surround themselves with people who are smart and independent thinkers, but who still show respect for the boss.

Fear of failure also creates motivation, according to former House Minority Leader Richard Gephardt. When you are running for office every two years, you have that fear of failure with you all the time, Congressman Gephardt says. But a good politician uses that concern to motivate himself or herself to keep on top of all of the issues. Similarly, according to ex-prosecutor and leading Democrat Ed Dowd, the fear of failure "results in preparation." No one wants to be embarrassed in court or giving a speech, so you should "internalize your fears" and use them to motivate you to be well-prepared for anything that you set out to do. Once you feel prepared, the fear evaporates.

Finally, you cannot let other people see your fear. Former Senator Alan Simpson notes that "fear and excitement or enthusiasm give off exactly the same body language." So, part of the process of harnessing fear for your advantage is to make it look like enthusiasm for tackling the new challenges ahead.

Invincible executives do not lie awake at night sweating. They do not allow their fears to paralyze them into timidity or inaction. Rather, they convert fear into sharper thinking, open communication, and reliance upon strong, reliable subordinates. If you let your fears sharpen your information-gathering and analytic skills, more often than not, "you will know the answer before you even start" down a particular road, says former Senator Bob Dole. According to Senator Dole, harnessing fear for positive ends puts you so much on top of a situation that you can live your career without ever asking a question to which the answer will be no. Your fear can lead you to sharpened levels of fact gathering and analysis such that you can eliminate most risks.

13

Respect Ambition, but Destroy Opportunism

> 📷 **SNAPSHOT**
>
> Are you good at spotting people who are trying to take advantage of you?
>
> **Yes:** 90 percent   **No:** 10 percent

"Show me a person without ambition and I'll show you a person who is going nowhere," Senator Bob Dole told me. Invincible executives love ambitious people. They reward ambitious people. They never feel threatened by ambitious people. But there is a fine line between ambition and opportunism. Cross that line and you are dead meat.

In April of 2002, I interviewed Earl Graves, the founder of *Black Enterprise* magazine and one of the most successful African-American entrepreneurs in the United States today. Mr. Graves's own career provides extensive insight into what creates an invincible executive—he rose from his beginnings as the poor son of Caribbean immigrants to earn a seat in boardrooms that symbolize American economic power. Not only is Mr. Graves's personal experience valuable to distilling the qualities of invincible executives, but he works so closely with other top executives across the country that he provided extensive insights into the inner workings of other top executives as well.

Mr. Graves started as an assistant to the late Robert F. Kennedy and currently sits on the board of DaimlerChrysler and many other top companies. Like so many top executives, Mr. Graves is direct and to the point—just a courteous tinge shy of abrupt. For example, I asked Mr. Graves, "How do you tell if someone you are considering for a job is going to be a good employee?" I expected a long analysis of the qualities that make productive employees. Instead, Mr. Graves responded, "If his first question is 'How many credit cards am I going to have?' this guy is not going to make it."

I asked the same question of former Senator Bob Dole in the political context. "How do you tell if a politician is opportunistic or sincere?" He replied: "Yell, 'Mr. President!' and watch how fast they turn around."

At the end of the last chapter, we discussed how top managers harness their fears into more precise professional conduct. A significant part of that sharpened professional awareness goes into picking high-quality, reliable people. The vast majority of invincible executives believe that they are good at separating the good employees from the bad ones, and good business partners from bad ones. They exhibit piercing discernment in their evaluation of other people—principally employees, but also potential customers, partners, and suppliers. Here is how they go about rewarding ambition and rooting out opportunism.

Gut Feeling

About half of the invincible executives with whom I discussed the issue claimed to have near clairvoyance in determining who will try to take advantage of them. "I can just tell by looking at them," or "I can tell after five minutes of speaking with them," was the variation on a theme I heard during my interviews. For example,

Bruno Schmitter, the CEO of the successful Hydromat, Inc, a major international supplier of high-tech machining equipment, told me: "I break people down like machines. I determine quickly whether they are reliable and consistent. I can see behind people who are not genuine and who do not have themselves under control." An executive trainer with whom I worked in the retail business several years ago echoed that sentiment: "A top executive separates ambition from opportunism almost immediately. We like ambition; we detest opportunism, and we are very good at telling the difference between the two," he said. If you are going to be an executive with staying power, therefore, you must value ambition, destroy opportunism, and be adept at telling the difference between the two.

Surprisingly, a few of the top executives I interviewed stated to me that they feel women are better than men at judging opportunism. Top banker and baseball team owner Drew Baur, for example, said that when he needs a quick, reliable judgment on someone's intentions, he asks his top women advisers for their opinions. "Women are simply better judges of opportunism than men," according to Baur. "We have had at the bank a couple of misfits, and I would have to say that some of the women executives picked it up much faster than I did."

There is probably some truth to the notion that top managers display good intuition about the quality of other people. But I suspect that, more often than not, what is really going on is the rapid assimilation of a variety of more concrete indicators of people who will not be reliable. Here are some of the more specific qualities that invincible executives seek in deciding the people and companies with whom they will work.

Quirks with Perks

Mr. Graves's story related earlier illustrates point number one. Invincible executives search for small, tangible signs of opportunism in those they are evaluating. Graves points to two such signs of an opportunistic person. First, opportunists make little slipups that show a preoccupation with "perks." An opportunist cannot help but think of himself or herself as being above the organization. Consequently, he or she will ask about company credit cards, flying first class, baseball tickets, fancy hotels. "They love to talk about these things; they can't help it," says Graves. That is not to say that people should never talk about the trappings of wealth and power. But invincible executives are on the lookout for people who are *preoccupied* with the perks—like new employees who raise these matters during their first few days at work, or seasoned employees who spend more time trying to get their airline seat upgraded than preparing for the meeting that necessitated the travel.

Second, Graves looks for someone who tries to change the organization before he or she understands it. He points to a new employee who immediately pushed for casual Fridays. She did not bother to find out that Mr. Graves is adamantly opposed to casual dress in the office. "Change is fine," he said, but "you do yourself a disservice to walk into an organization that is doing well and start imposing your values on it immediately." Opportunists try to mold everything to suit their personal desires, and they usually lack the patience to wait very long to do so.

Mike Sears of Boeing notes a third quirk of opportunists—the "spotlight" mentality. Opportunists are pleasant and charming when the spotlight is on; they are irritable, condescending, and moody when they are toiling behind the scenes. Look for these signs.

The Buck Stops Over There Somewhere

Others who are good at picking out opportunists look for an opportunist's specific choice of words rather than focusing on the subject matter of the person's communications or his or her general attitude. For example, opportunists take credit for all victories.

They are not the conduit for the organization—a concept that we discussed earlier. Consequently, they use "I" and "me" instead of "we" when discussing positive results or developments.

They also remind others constantly of their victories—even when the organization has moved on to new matters. Opportunists feel a need to tell you—in the first five minutes of any given conversation—about some great victory they had, some important title they had, some board they sit on, or someone important they know. Ambitious people, on the other hand, allow others to tell you about their accomplishments and then downplay these accomplishments when you bring them up.

The self-centered words, phrases, and stories that characterize an opportunist disappear when problems arise. In these situations, opportunists tend to compartmentalize their jobs in order to limit their exposure to failure. First, they try to avoid assignments that carry with them a significant risk of failure—even when such situations present a great opportunity for success as well. "Opportunists shy away from risk, even when there are large potential rewards. The reason is simple. They plan to jump back into the risky matter once they are confident that everything will turn out well," according to seasoned corporate attorney Jack Walbran.

When failure does occur or seems imminent, opportunists run for cover quickly. That includes shirking responsibility for the actions of their subordinates. Consequently, they frequently use phrases like "you'll have to check with Susan" or "unfortunately, my assistant did not get that done." They pass the buck at the very first opportunity. Many go so far as to send subordinates into "bad" meetings, even when their own peers will be present.

A senior Justice Department official once told me that his least favorite phrase from a subordinate is "should be." "For example, I assign you and your legal team to do a 'white paper' on an important legal strategy. A week later I ask you if the white paper on the new legal strategy is done, and you answer, 'Should be.' That phrase says three things about you. First, the phrase says that you think I am too stupid to figure out that you do not know the answer to my question. You do not know if the paper is done or not and you won't admit it. That is patronizing. Second, the phrase 'should be' says you do not know what your people are doing. You have not taken the time to interact with your subordinates to determine if they have completed the assignment. Finally, the phrase says that you are ready to blame someone else if the job hasn't been done. You are 'predistancing' yourself from the failure. That's why the phrase 'should be' is a sure sign of both ineptitude and opportunism at work."

Aptitude and Attitude

Many invincible executives require that new hires take intelligence and psychological tests. Sam Fox of the Harbour Group told me that his company simply will not hire *anyone*, even a receptionist, who is not in the ninety-ninth percentile of all college graduates in intelligence. "There is no substitute for intelligence and integrity," says Fox. One of the main reasons people cut corners in business is that they are not smart enough to get the job done right. So they look for little ways to compensate for their intellectual shortcomings. It may be by taking credit for someone else's work. It may be by saying they completed an assignment that they in fact have not completed. It may involve stretching the truth or the law. A lot of opportunism that you see in the workplace is a cover for incompetence.

Energy and Attitude

Wait a minute! There are a lot of opportunistic employees and coworkers who are really smart, aren't there? In fact, the stereotypical corporate opportunist is a highly intelligent, conniving SOB, right?

Sometimes, but less often than you would think. Most opportunists are clever but vacuous—they have mastered the art of appearance but exhibit very little depth. Keep in mind what we said earlier—invincible executives admire ambition. Often what separates an ambitious person from an opportunist is intelligence. Smart people see the whole picture, so they realize that long-term success requires a commitment to the organization and hard work. Opportunists, on the other hand, try to get more than they deserve, which often means using underhanded tactics to leverage their intellectual shortcomings.

There are exceptions—i.e., situations where intelligent people become opportunists. One is where the smart person is downright lazy. People who focus on the "flash" rather than the "sweat equity" will eventually be exposed, according to Joe Ryan, executive vice president at Marriott. If a smart person does not like to work, he or she will cut corners, just like a person who is in over his or her head intellectually. Stupidity and laziness are one and the same as far as the effect on the organization. Consequently, invincible executives keep their eyes on the lookout for people who come in late or leave early, who always take the maximum number of days off allowed, who find excuses not to work extra hours or weekends when the job demands it. Again, this is more than a question of work ethic; it is a sign of a potential opportunist.

The Honesty Check

Finally, invincible executives—even those who feel they have good intuition—do exhaustive background checks on those with whom they are considering working—employees as well as customers and suppliers. They know that 30 percent of résumés have material misrepresentations on them. That includes high-level people. An Illinois circuit judge had to resign recently because he had lied about receiving the Medal of Honor. The football coach at Notre Dame resigned in 2001 because he had lied about his prior playing and coaching experience. If you want to be invincible professionally, you must verify the integrity of those with whom you are entrusting your career.

It is surprising (and unfortunate) how many people hire or do business with others based upon an interview, a meeting, or by taking a résumé or marketing brochure at face value. To protect your own career, you need to verify independently the facts people provide you about themselves or their companies. There is so much information available about other people and organizations—much of it online through LexisNexis, Internet websites, and government agencies from police departments to the Securities and Exchange Commission—that there is no excuse anymore for doing business with a bad egg. Invincible executives check out every fact on a résumé. Invincible executives verify every representation in a marketing brochure. They do criminal background checks and study the litigation history of any prospective employee or business associate. They investigate the financial history of prospective trading partners. They do ethics investigations into financial and legal advisers to see if they have ever been professionally disciplined.

If a person lies to get a job, he will lie to keep it and will lie when he sues you after you fire him. If a supplier lies to get your business, he will lie when he cannot perform, and he will lie when you sue him for it. Most of the time, the professional histories of these people and companies will tip you off that they are opportunistic. Do not take the statements of those who want to work with you at face value.

RULE

14

Value Loyalty, but Do Not Depend on It

📷 SNAPSHOT

Do you require loyalty to you and your company or organization?

Very much so: 30 percent **Not essential:** 70 percent

The typical American college student who graduates in the year 2003 will have twelve to fifteen jobs in his or her forty-five years in the workforce. This simple fact about the employment world today dictates that you cannot expect long-term loyalty from your employees.

Thirty years ago, it was quite common for employees to spend their entire careers at one organization. The reason was simple: loyalty was a two-way street back then. Companies had a policy of "employment for life," according to Mike Sears of Boeing. Your company would virtually guarantee you a job, so the company, in turn, expected you to stay with the company until retirement. No more. With the new corporate environment—global, fast-paced, and cutthroat—companies must always consider downsizing, outsourcing, mergers, and layoffs to keep their competitive edge—all of which means that your company can no longer guarantee you a job. Now, according to Sears, the best and most conscientious companies guarantee only "employability for life"—meaning that you will learn skills that you can transfer to other companies or industries if your own company cannot keep you. That shift in emphasis from "employment for life" to "employability for life" changes the dynamics of professional loyalty significantly.

Loyalty with a Little "L"

Since companies have downsized their loyalty to their employees, managers must also downsize the loyalty that they expect from their employees. The "Big L" loyalty demanded from employees of the past was an undying, patriotic, and almost spiritual commitment to the company for a lifetime. Those days are gone. Rather, in return for the new, limited promise of employability, you have the right to expect employees to remain loyal only with a little "L."

Loyalty with a little "L" means little more than a commitment to put the company's interest first while you work there. Invincible executives, therefore, expect their employees to refrain from such activities as insider trading, antitrust or anticompetitive actions, bribery and kickbacks, pirating software, harassment and discrimination, and other illegal or unethical acts showing that personal interests or the interests of others are more important than those of the company. Successful executives also have a right to expect that employees do not do personal activities on company time, do not lie about lateness or sickness, and refrain from other activities that, while not serious legal infractions, cost the company money. The only loyalty that an invincible executive expects from an employee is that the employee do his or her job ethically and well.

But that is the extent of it. Sure, it is wonderful to have employees who wave the company flag at all times, and those employees should be rewarded. But the invincible executive does not expect or require that sort of loyalty from employees to the organization because he or she cannot guarantee a reciprocal level of loyalty by the organization to the employee.

True Believers and Forced Believers

In this context, there are two means by which invincible executives protect the interest of their companies over the interests of individual employees—and these two means are diametrically opposed to one another. They develop "core loyalists" and "contract loyalists."

First, the invincible executive develops a few true believers—core loyalists. Executives who enjoy long-term success always have a personal charisma that inspires loyalty. Unfortunately, there are a limited number of people top executives can get to know well enough to make them true believers. So the most successful professionals focus their efforts to build true loyalty with a few very talented people. Indeed, virtually every top professional I interviewed said that he or she had a handful of long-term confidants whom he or she could trust entirely. They may be older mentors, younger protégés, or trusted contemporaries—and are often a mix of the three. But it is unlikely that in an entire career you will be able to find and cultivate more than five such people, and it is a waste of time to attempt more.

That's when the more Machiavellian side of the invincible executive steps in. Top professionals force loyalty where they cannot earn it. They do it through three mechanisms: (1) employment agreements, (2) confidentiality pacts, and (3) covenants not to sue. This is contract loyalty.

Invincible executives value employment contracts. They get such contracts for themselves, and they require their top talent to sign them as well. An employment agreement defines loyalty as a matter of law, not a matter of organizational patriotism. The agreement

specifies the pay, benefits, and severance that the employee gets—
that is the company's guaranteed loyalty to the employee. But the
agreement also contains clauses that prohibit the employee from
working for competitors in specified geographic areas for specified
periods of time after he or she leaves—that is the employee's forced
loyalty to the company. State laws govern the extent to which you
can preclude a former employee from competing with you, but
there is a lot of leeway to do so, and invincible executives take maximum advantage of their ability to restrict top talent from competing with them in the future.

Next, invincible executives require all employees at all levels to
sign confidentiality agreements at the time they start work. These
agreements define the type of information that the company deems
to be proprietary, and the agreements preclude employees from disclosing this information outside the company—even after the
employee leaves the company. Confidentiality agreements also
require employees to promise to not take any company documents
or electronic files with them when they depart.

Finally, top executives seek waivers of legal liability from departing employees. The rules on obtaining such waivers are tricky and
require legal counsel, but they have become an essential part of
doing business successfully these days. So many executives—even
very senior ones—are done in by disgruntled former employees
that top managers have become very familiar with legal waivers and
the necessity of using them at all possible times. Often the company will offer a more attractive severance package in exchange for
the departing employee's promise not to initiate any sort of legal
action against the company. Some companies also elicit statements
that the employee is unaware of any illegal or unethical conduct
that occurred at the company while the employee was there.
Remember, however, that there is a fine line between getting an
honest statement of exoneration and looking like you are paying to

sweep problems under the rug, so waivers of this type should be negotiated and drafted by professionals.

The standard for professional loyalty has changed with the times. Most of today's invincible executives neither show pervasive loyalty to their employees, nor do they expect it from them. However, they do require observance of basic integrity and professionalism. Then, they cultivate a small core of true believers. And finally, top professionals use contractual mechanisms to protect their organizations in an era when you can no longer depend upon traditional notions of loyalty to do so.

RULE

15

Put a Very Fine Line Between Yourself and Your Subordinates

📷 SNAPSHOT

Do you deliberately keep professional distance from your superiors, subordinates, and/or peers?

Usually: 52 percent   **Usually not:** 48 percent

As the top law enforcement officer in the country, Janet Reno did not regularly socialize with her Department of Justice attorneys. She occasionally went out with her prosecutors when they celebrated a successful conviction or civil settlement. While she treated everyone at Justice with cordiality and pleasant professionalism, and she was very popular with her employees, she deliberately kept some distance between herself and her subordinates. You need "just enough of a wall to provide for the dignity of the office," according to Ms. Reno. However, there must be "enough caring" that employees can see "around, through, and under the wall, and through the windows," she added.

Admiral Joseph Prueher agrees. "When you are in command, you are not one of the boys anymore. You are in charge. You can be friendly, you can be helpful, and you can put your arm around them when times are tough. But you are not one of them. And that has got to come across."

One of Ms. Reno's top prosecutors, former U.S. Attorney Ed Dowd, took a different approach to leading his office. He treated his prosecutors, administrative staff, and investigative agents as if they were all part of his family. He had them over for dinner; he attended their social events and celebrations on a very regular basis. Businessmen Sam Fox and Mike Sears, both of whom we met earlier, told me that they develop close ties to coworkers and subordinates, although Sears does not go so far as to use the word "family."

Similarly, when I asked Jim Parker, CEO of Southwest Airlines, whether he keeps professional distance from his employees, he replied, "Absolutely not. That would be totally counter to the culture at Southwest." Parker, who does view his company as one big family, recounted stories of his icing down the beer at after-hours company "deck parties" on Fridays, and otherwise spending a lot of time socializing with his employees. In fact, of the forty top professionals I interviewed, Mr. Parker was the only one who took me into his office (around 6:15 P.M., after most people had left), opened a bottle of merlot, and poured me some very good wine into a plastic cup. We sipped it throughout the interview. I saw the value of professional congeniality firsthand. It certainly can and has worked at Southwest.

The Friendship Trade-Off

The question of how close you become to coworkers—particularly subordinates—is a very tricky one. There is no consensus among invincible executives on this point. A business enterprise that is run like a family has unique benefits—greater employee enthusiasm, a more synergistic spirit and sense of mission, and a lot of laughing and fun. These characteristics can inspire great productivity. Several invincible executives noted to me that family-style enterprises tend to have less employee turnover, which means greater efficiency. Hendrik Verfaillie, former CEO of Monsanto, believes that "the benefit of having friends and relationships in the company outweighs the negative situations, where you have to fire a friend, for example." Workers who develop close professional friendships with superiors and subordinates are more likely to be willing to stay late or come in on weekends when the company is in a crunch. They are also more willing to make pay and benefit sacrifices when times are bad.

But there is a downside. Doug Bain of Boeing, while maintaining upbeat and respectful relationships with his subordinates, agrees with those who say that you have to keep some professional distance from those who work for you. He notes that he has never had a party for coworkers at his home. If you get too close to your employees, it becomes very painful to have a "difficult conversation" with them about their professional situation. It is, for example, much harder to fire or demote a nonproductive employee if you have treated that person as a close friend or family member. Richard Bell, CEO of HDR, Inc, agrees: "Absolutely, I keep a distance. I am cordial. I talk with them. But I do not think that the boss has to sit right in the middle of them and be one of the gang." You have to keep some distance, albeit in a pleasant and professional manner, according to Bell. Besides, he notes, "they need their own time."

Close friends often become overly emotional during times of crisis—which is a major cause of the breakup of family businesses. In addition, disparities in compensation or promotions among "family-style" employees tend to get blown out of proportion. And close friendships between employees and customers or suppliers often lead to the employees compromising the best interests of their companies.

I have heard several struggling executives complain that their secretaries and assistants stopped taking them seriously after they made concerted efforts to treat their staff members like friends and equals. "They started to feel like they could get away with long lunches, doing a lot of personal things on company time—that kind of stuff," a senior manager of a management consulting firm lamented to me. "Then, when I tried to bring the issue up, they resented me for it," he added. "The whole situation became too emotionally charged—and I attribute that fact to my own insistence that everyone be part of a professional family rather than a professional organization." In fact, two mid-level managers told me that, after unsuccessful attempts at the "we're all friends" approach, they reverted to having their new staff assistants call them "Mr." rather than by their first names. "Keeping it formal simply took some of the unpredictability out of my job, so it was worth it," one of them confided to me.

Creative Solution

Both the "friendship" and the "distance" approaches have their plusses and minuses. So what is the best approach? Perhaps a compromise between the two is the safest style. There are some executives who seem to have developed relationships with subordinates and coworkers that allow them to enjoy the best of both scenarios. They get the positive attitude spawned by friendship and the discipline that tends to grow out of corporate formality. Interestingly, the people who have achieved this balance tend to come from either the most open and creative professional disciplines, such as the entertainment industry, or the most rigid professions, such as the military. But their advice would seem to be instructive in the more traditional business world as well.

On the entertainment side, Sheryl Crow, Chris Lloyd, and Earl Graves (who are at the top of the music, television, and publishing industries respectively) made some interesting and similar observations in this regard. Crow works with musicians, singers, roadies, and engineers with the objective of producing a highly creative song or concert. Graves and Lloyd work with talented writers who are paid to come up with uniquely creative ideas. But all of that unstructured creativity has to be channeled into producing a final, highly structured product—a twelve-song record, a monthly magazine, a thirty-minute sitcom. Imposing structure on creative impulses requires the development of professional relationships that carefully balance a sense of familial emotion with one of professional organization.

Here is how they do it. First and foremost, "Everyone has to know who is the boss," says Earl Graves. There can be no pretense that everyone is equal in terms of where they are in the organization. If you tell everyone that there are no differences between you and them, they feel no need or sense of urgency to do what you tell them to do. That can be a tough way to manage people—especially in a creative field. Lloyd agrees. Writers putting together a sitcom story line need to know that the executive producer makes the final decision relative to disagreements in the direction that the story is going, and after the decision is made, people must channel their creative energies in the direction that the executive producer dictates. In order to achieve this discipline within a creative endeavor, employees should never be allowed to cultivate the false premise that everyone on the job is equal or equally important. It is just not true. If it were, nothing would ever get done. Sheryl Crow said virtually the same thing: "I am running the business. . . . I am the one calling the shots."

This kind of buy-in to the hierarchy is, of course, the lynchpin of a military organization as well. "Everyone has to show a total understanding and commitment to the relative ranks of the people in the organization," a special operations officer told me during my stint as a federal prosecutor. However, even a military officer agrees that bosses who simply proclaim their higher position and then demand deference are rarely successful over the long term. "There is an important difference between having subordinates who show deference and having subordinates who exhibit true respect," the officer noted. Haughty officers who constantly remind their soldiers who is the boss get soldiers who are deferential—meaning that the employees treat them with an Eddie Haskell–like, phony sense of respect. Behind the scenes, however, employees with bosses who demand deference make snide comments, cut corners, and scan the want ads.

That is where the personal element finds its limited but important place in the professional hierarchy. You earn the respect of your employees, not only by showing professional skill and accomplishment, but also by showing personal and genuine concern for their well-being. For example, Lieutenant General Sams agrees that "there needs to be a clear dividing line between the commander and the troops." However, he also recognizes the extreme importance of making personal connections with the people working for you. How does he do it? "The best way to make a person feel good about himself or herself," according to General Sams, "is to pick up the phone, call that person's spouse, and tell their spouse what a great job the person is doing. In fact, if you keep a little distance— which you really have to do in the military and ought to do in other fields too—then when you do make that call to the spouse, it means a lot more. If you are out there having beers with them every day and trying to be liked, the call actually means less."

Sheryl Crow has a similar viewpoint. She notes that when you take a crew out on the road with you, "in a way it is a bit like a company because you are asking people to give a piece of themselves. And you want them to feel comfortable, to give the best of themselves. . . . So my touring band, I think they feel well appreciated, but at the same time, they know who is the boss."

Bill Marriott agrees. He notes that "if you take good care of your employees, they will take good care of the customer." This is not a calculating process. Your motives must be sincere. You learn about your employees out of a true appreciation for those whose professional lives are at least in part devoted to supporting you.

Perhaps Earl Graves put the concept most succinctly when he said, "I do not try to make employees members of my family. I try to keep a certain distance because familiarity all the time is not the best approach to business. But I do get involved. I take an interest in their careers and families. If you do those kinds of things for people, they are going to be there for you."

Don't Fake Friendship

As you can see, top executives can care about their employees without purporting to become close friends with them. More important, the worst thing you can do is to pretend you are close to your employees—a mistake many executives make. People can detect phony acts of ingratiation. If you are insincere, you will make mistakes that give you away.

I remember, for example, when Senator Danforth interviewed President Clinton in connection with his investigation into the Waco tragedy. At the time, President Clinton was in the middle of Ken Starr's independent counsel investigation and was understandably wary of yet another investigator looking into his conduct. But the president tried to defuse the situation with calculating ingratiation. During the interview Senator Danforth naturally addressed President Clinton as "Mr. President." However, throughout the interview President Clinton referred to Senator Danforth as "John" in a tone of voice that suggested that they had been friends for years. In fact, the president's first words were, "John! Nice to talk to you." The problem was that no one who knows Senator Danforth calls him John. Everyone calls him Jack. The whole exchange was colored negatively by the repeated references to "John." Senator Danforth never said anything about it, but several of his staffers who were present felt that the calculated effort at ingratiation did not help the president at all.

The lowest-risk, highest-yield leveraging of relationships with subordinates, therefore, involves setting up a basic hierarchical structure in which everyone has a realistic sense of his or her importance to the organization. That must be supplemented with genuine, sincere efforts by the people at the top to get to know about the lives and priorities of those working for them. While everyone is not equal, everyone must know how much his or her contributions mean to the organization. Finally, top managers have to be willing to go the extra mile to help subordinates in the organization to improve their professional and personal standing. If you tell people "I appreciate you and the sacrifices you make, and I will help you improve your professional life," you do not have to adopt the phony pretense that everyone is at an equal position in the organization.

In sum, employees have a right to expect that you care about their lives. While you do not have to pretend that a roadie is as important to the enterprise as the singer-songwriter, and you do not have your workers over for dinner every month, you should appreciate that your needs and requirements affect, alter, and sometimes disrupt their lives. The very least they can expect is that you get to know the names of their spouses and kids, you go out of your way to talk to them when they are around, and you help them along with their careers and personal crises when you have the opportunity.

A Lesson from Foreign Minds

Two of the people I interviewed for this book—Bruno Schmitter (CEO of Hydromat) and Hendrik Verfaillie (former CEO of Monsanto) were born and raised in Europe. They both adopt an approach to professional friendship that is similar to that advocated above—keeping a little professional distance from their employees based on the reality of the need for business hierarchy, supplemented with genuine and personalized concern for the well-being of their employees. But they add one important dimension to the analysis that comes from their foreign upbringing. Effective American executives recognize hierarchy, but, unlike their European counterparts, they also recognize that everyone has a chance to move up in that hierarchy. So, while superiors keep some distance between themselves and their subordinates, a critical factor in the success of American organizations is that the subordinates all have the chance to advance.

"Europe is extremely hierarchical . . . and I just despised that," notes Schmitter. In Germany, you might work side by side with the same boss for thirty years and you still have to use the formal pronouns when addressing the boss. You will probably not know all that much about your boss's family, and he or she will not know too much about yours. It is almost as if there is a managerial class and a working class, and there is no effort to find common ground between the two.

The rigid sense of hierarchy lowered the professional expectations and social mobility of employees. Working-class families tended to stay working-class families. "When I was younger, I just did not feel comfortable with the habits of my friends. After school, you go to the local tavern or restaurant and have a few beers and go home, and the next day you start all over. I wanted to see more," noted Schmitter.

Verfaillie and Schmitter believe that one of the best characteristics of American business or industry is that the concept of "permanent" hierarchy is less prevalent. Just because your father was a miner does not mean that you have to be one. A corporate structure never becomes a detention cell for people of certain social and economic backgrounds. Having seen a European system that is less mobile and slower to react to changing situations, both Verfaillie and Schmitter make a concerted effort to look for talent and ability at all levels and in all areas of their companies. They pride themselves on their ability to ignore the social backgrounds of their employees. They take a special interest in the careers of those who have overcome adversity, and they work hard to bring them up in the corporate structure. They also see their efforts to promote talented people as contributing to the broader goal of improving social mobility in the society as a whole. As Verfaillie put it, "It became clear to me that an American company gave much better chances to people to advance than in Europe. . . . In America it was much more based on performance and skill."

Perhaps Barrett Toan, the visionary CEO of Express Scripts, summed the issue of professional distance best when he told me, "The relationship you want to develop with your people is one of trust, not friendship." If they understand you and see your good intentions, and if you give them the opportunity to improve their professional lives, they will respect you and you will get good work out of them. You do not, however, need to become their best friend.

16

Wield a Spiritual Shield, but Not a Spiritual Sword

┌─ **📷 SNAPSHOT** ──────────────────────────┐

What role does religious or spiritual faith play in your
professional life?

Major: 12 percent   **Minor:** 88 percent
└──────────────────────────────────────┘

There are top executives and politicians who make a direct appeal
to God every day, asking him to help them make the right professional decisions. Attorney General Ashcroft has a prayer meeting
every morning at work for those who want to participate. Supreme
Court Justice Clarence Thomas also uses his faith to help him guide
and plan the important decisions in his career. Football quarter-
back Kurt Warner of the Super Bowl–winning Rams weaves his
Christian beliefs into nearly any interview he does, and directly
attributes his meteoric rise to football greatness to his faith in God.

Others, while not using "religion" per se in their professional
lives, believe that their success has a seriously spiritual dimension.
Hollywood agent Joel Gotler does not adhere to organized religion,
but he discussed the importance of spiritual balance with me at

least a dozen times in a ninety-minute interview. Similarly, Sheryl Crow believes that the breaks that she got in reaching the top, while not necessarily inspired by God, were part of some larger plan for her life.

Greed, Pride, and God

Then there is the other extreme. Many successful people keep religion and/or spirituality out of their professional lives entirely. Janet Reno put this view most succinctly when she told me: "It is *my* religious and spiritual world. It is very much a part of me. And I never inject it or permit it to be injected into my professional life."

Some go even further than Ms. Reno and actually criticize the use of religion in the professional world. Richard Parker, a Harvard Law professor who taught me constitutional law many years ago, used words roughly to this effect to describe his dislike for professionals who spend a lot of time talking about God: "Let's face it, to most people, the purpose of a career is to make money and/or gain some notoriety. Even in those professions like research, university teaching, and politics—where the money is bad—you have incredible battles of pride and ego—perhaps even more so than in the corporate world. To give God any credit or role whatsoever in that kind of cutthroat professional environment is hypocritical." According to Professor Parker, because greed and/or pride are two essential elements for professional success, to say that God got you there is a slap in the face to anyone who really believes in religion.

It is hard to dispute that a lot of very nasty people have gone far in the business world. However, as we discussed earlier and will discuss later, truly invincible executives display such qualities as care for their employees, contrition when they make mistakes, and other qualities that display an underlying morality. So perhaps the professor's view of the role of spirituality in the workplace is a bit too cynical.

But the professor does have one point that we must address squarely: most businesspeople have to do some pretty mean things to stay on top. So is there a place for sincere spirituality in a professional life? Do you need to "compartmentalize" your job and your faith? Or do you play "tag team"—as one software executive once put it—using your after-hours confessional to mop up some of the bad things you did during the workweek?

The Spiritual Sword

Based on my interviews and professional experiences, executives who wear their religions on their sleeves are incurring unnecessary professional risk. Overt references to religion during business discussions can alienate customers and coworkers who are of a different faith. I have heard Jewish executives say that they feel very put off when senior executives make references to Christ in connection with business transactions. "How am I supposed to react when the boss asks Jesus for help in closing a deal and then sends me to draft the terms and conditions?" a Jewish corporate attorney at a Fortune 500 company once asked me.

I had several discussions by telephone with a man named "Sammy" after my last book came out. I met him initially when he called in on a syndicated AP radio show, and he followed up by calling me at my office a couple of times. Sammy was a Muslim of Arab descent who worked for a software company. After September 11, 2001, he noted a marked increase in discussions about Christ and Christianity among certain coworkers when he was around. He believed that these discussions were not sincere expressions of faith in times of trouble, but something more nefarious—a deliberate attempt to alienate him. Soon, according to Sammy, the comments moved from being pro-Christian to anti-Muslim. Then he was let go as the result of a downsizing initiative. He claims that it was religious prejudice that cost him his job.

From the facts I heard, it was hard to say whether Sammy was the victim of prejudice or whether he misinterpreted some post-9/11 spiritual patriotism on the part of his coworkers. However, the mere ambiguity of the situation makes an important point to would-be invincible executives. If you, in a business context, make comments that suggest that you value one religion over another, you are leaving yourself open to charges of favoritism, or even discrimination. Sammy's situation represents a very common fact pattern in civil rights lawsuits filed by terminated employees against senior executives. Juries have a tough time telling the difference between a proper termination for valid reasons and improper religious discrimination in any situation where the professional context shows a preference toward a particular religion. You should not leave yourself open to these kinds of charges.

The lesson for aspiring professionals is clear. Do not use religion as a sword in the workplace or you risk alienating employees upon whom you rely. Moreover, you open yourself unnecessarily to charges of favoritism and discrimination.

The Spiritual Shield

While using religion as a professional sword often results in a backlash of resentment and allegations of favoritism, most of the executives I interviewed found some role for spirituality in their professional lives. While they do not make religious proclamations at work, they also reject the notion that they must compartmentalize their religious and their professional lives. Rather, they use their religion as a shield. "It is an individual thing," says Joe Ryan of Marriott. "It is important professionally but not necessarily for the public to see." Or, as Mike Sears of Boeing put it, "It is a backdrop, it's values, it's you—but it is not tied directly into how you run your business."

This shield manifests itself in several ways. First, religion provides a moral context in which to make business decisions, according to Jack Danforth. You go to church or temple, and that immersion in faith reminds you of the values by which you must conduct both your personal and your professional life—fairness, accountability, and respect for other people. These qualities are not constraints upon professional success, but rather means to professional invincibility. In that sense, religion protects you from making the big mistakes that can destroy careers—serving, as I said, as a shield rather than a sword.

However, you also use your religious beliefs to temper your competitive nature—to keep you from relying too much upon money or power as a measure of success in life. You develop, for example, the faith-based qualities of generosity and charity. Virtually every invincible executive devotes countless hours to raising money for charities and community causes, and many attribute this activity to lessons that they learned from religious teachings.

Religion also gives you a perspective that assists in strategic decision making, according to Bill Marriott. "Religion gives you the long-term look at things. In business, everything is 'today'—you've got ten catastrophes going on at once. Then you go home at night and you have to take an eternal perspective. Where am I going to be years from now? That's where religion comes in."

The Benefits of Doing Good

This discussion of the religious shield is more than just moralistic context. I do not think it is blasphemous to acknowledge that religious activities have their tactical advantages as well. Few executives—even those who are very successful in purely business endeavors—jump to "invincible" status without tremendous community visibility. Not only does religion provide a moral impetus for becoming involved in charitable community activity, but it also provides the vehicle for attaining community visibility. Religious charities tend to be run by boards of directors that resemble a Who's Who of any given community. By participating in them when you are young, you can make strong contacts that can help you advance your career—at least to a limited extent. Executives have told me that many of their customer and client relationships started with a meeting in connection with the activities of a charitable organization. It has happened to me on several occasions, as it has to several invincible executives with whom I discussed the issue.

Moreover, as you move up the professional ladder, you will find that charities love to reward their most successful supporters with awards and publicity. You should eat this up! As long as PR is not your primary motive, you should feel no moral dilemma whatsoever in getting something back from an organization to which you have given a great deal of time and/or money. The key to getting the most out of such a situation is to remember that religion is a shield, meaning that you never push for publicity or recognition. Let it come to you—as it certainly will—because recognition does not cost a charity anything.

Use Your Spirituality to Maintain Professional Balance

Another aspect of the spiritual shield is that religion is a vehicle for atonement. Invincible executives sometimes have to be ruthless. In most cases, this ruthlessness may be both professionally and morally justifiable. But there will undoubtedly be times when you realize that you have gone too far in your treatment of rivals or adversaries. Your religion may have a formal means to atone for a loss of equilibrium—such as a Catholic confessional or a Jewish holiday like Yom Kippur—or you may rely upon simple prayer to seek a return to moral balance when you have strayed. In either event, having such a vehicle does more than score points with God. It also provides you a counterweight that keeps your professional life in a low-risk zone. There can be little doubt that if you get away with underhanded conduct and have no countervailing force in your life, your professional direction will tend toward scandal. Once again, religion is the shield that protects you from a downward spiral of professional unscrupulousness.

Finally, invincible executives draw on their faith for strength in times of trouble. "You learn where to turn when you do not know where to turn," according to former Senator Alan Simpson. And where you turn is inward, to your spiritual side, he notes. For example, Tom Gunn, a senior aerospace executive and consultant, told me that religion played little role in his professional life until he learned that he was under investigation for alleged improper conduct in connection with sales of aircraft to the U.S. Air Force and Navy. He knew he was innocent and, ultimately, was completely exonerated. But, early in the investigation, the federal government was closing in on him with search warrants and press leaks. It was during this crisis that he developed "a strong spiritual sense" without which "I would have never made it through the situation. And I have kept it to this day. And it is something that I didn't have before," he said. That is the power of the shield of faith.

RULE

17

You Do Not Have to Be Good-Looking, but You Have to Look Good

📷 **SNAPSHOT**

Do you think personal appearance is important to professional success?

Yes: 100 percent   **No:** 0 percent

Emmy-winning producer Christopher Lloyd spoke for the whole group of interviewees when he said, "A pleasant personal appearance is a plus. It is probably a failing of human nature, but I think people tend to like to be around attractive people—not necessarily physically attractive—just people who present themselves well." This view permeates every professional field. "You must have a pleasant demeanor and dress appropriately," according to Doug Bain of Boeing. Ron Gafford, CEO of Austin Industries, agrees that "appearance to the customer" and to your own people is an essential element of professional success. I got a similar reaction from virtually every one of the forty top professionals whom I interviewed.

This is a tough subject to discuss—so much so that a couple of the invincible executives I interviewed on the subject spoke only on the condition of anonymity. People want to believe that "inner beauty"—respect for others, intelligence, competence—are the most important elements to professional success. Unfortunately, the real and the ideal are quite different. The bottom line: a positive personal appearance is a critical element of lasting professional success. The opinion was unanimous.

Use What You've Got

The good news is that, while being "good-looking" is a definite plus, many people with average or below-average looks do well in the business world *as long as they do the best with what they have.* "I'm not looking for beauty," commented Juanita Hinshaw, the sharply dressed and sharp-looking CFO of the multibillion-dollar company Graybar Electric, "but primarily I want just neat, well-groomed people who dress appropriately for the occasion." Hinshaw and her peers at the top of the corporate world agree that you do not have to have movie star looks, but others have to perceive you as someone who makes every effort to look good.

At the other extreme, some employees seem to take pride in dressing down as much as possible. Bad idea. Earl Graves, publisher of *Black Enterprise* magazine, lamented to me that "I have people in my building who look like they are going to the beach." They will never work for him. "Sometimes there seems to be a competition for who can be the worst dressed and what they can get away with, you know, how sloppy can we be?" notes Juanita Hinshaw. She agrees with Graves that this approach is a very career-limiting move.

Good-Looking Is Good

While making the best of what you have is all you can do, let there be no doubt that certain physical characteristics provide advantages in the workplace. Senior male invincible executives tend to be tall, good-looking, well-proportioned, and not bald. (If it makes you feel any better, the author is one-for-four.) While few are grossly overweight, many are "big." In fact, Ron Gafford of Austin Industries told me a story about the CEO of a well-known construction company who, some years back, "only hired big people" because he thought he could intimidate the competition, and in some cases the clients, with a bunch of tall, tough-looking employees. Gafford, however, does not agree with this way of thinking.

Female invincible executives tend to be slightly more diverse in terms of height and traditional notions of "looks." After all, Janet Reno *gained* in popularity when she became the topic of personal appearance jokes. But in virtually all cases, top female executives are well-dressed, meticulously groomed, and not overweight. And most are very good-looking as well.

The comments that I heard on this subject were surprisingly candid. "Part of success is being in shape," according to Earl Graves. "I have never really met an overweight CEO," he added. "There may be some 'big' CEOs—you know 6'6", 270 pounds—but few if any have a poor height-to-weight ratio," according to Graves.

Diverse Good Looks

Bill Marriott is a true stickler for personal appearance, but he made it clear to me that his strong emphasis on appearance cannot be confused with the idea that only silver-haired, white males can rise to the top. He pointed out with pride that his company and the country as a whole have made great strides in promoting people of different races and cultural backgrounds. He considers the move away from white males as the only talent pool for top executives as a major positive development for the business world. But he, as others, acknowledged that there remains discrimination in favor of attractive-looking people at the top of the executive ranks—whatever their gender or ethnic background may be. Ethical top professionals will promote women, African-Americans, Muslims, Jews, Asians—anyone—but only if they have impeccable personal hygiene and appearance.

The silver lining here is that the immutable characteristics—i.e., genetic ones—are less important than the ones over which you have some control. For example, Senator Alan Simpson, a very tall man, conceded that his height has helped him. However, he also noted that former Labor Secretary Robert Reich, who is 4'10", is a "commanding presence" in a room. Sam Fox—who is 5'6"—has built a fortune worth hundreds of millions of dollars. He puts it this way: "As much as I would like to be 6'4", I am 4'18"—like it or not. I can't do anything about that! But I sure as hell have a lot to say about how often I get my hair cut, how often it is washed, that it is neatly combed, how often I shave, if I go out in the evening with a morning shave, if I have a suit that is crumpled and shoes that aren't shined. Those are some of the things over which I have absolute control. As for the things which I cannot control, I disregard them."

More important, if you lack certain of the immutable physical characteristics that help in achieving success, there are several ways in which you can overcome those disadvantages. First, however, you must take an honest look in the mirror and decide whether you have an appearance handicap. If so, you cannot ignore it, deny it, or become resigned to it. Any of those approaches will prevent you from becoming the invincible executive. Rather, you must confront your disadvantages on a characteristic by characteristic basis and develop a personal style that either downplays the disadvantage or, better yet, converts it into a strength. Let's explore how to maximize your personal appearance such that you are in the running to become professionally invincible.

The Owner-Founder Equation

There is one professional context in which appearance is all but irrelevant. Take a look at Bill Gates. He is a nerd. He has an awkward appearance and demeanor. He came across as petulant and childish in his deposition in the Microsoft antitrust trial. Yet I would say he did pretty well for himself. He is the greatest professional success story of the late twentieth century.

When you are the founder and owner of a business, it does not make much difference what you look like. I call this the "owner/ founder exception" to the rule that personal appearance is important to becoming professionally secure. Jack Schmitt, the car dealer we met earlier, agrees. Being the owner, or the son or daughter of the owner, renders personal appearance of minimal importance in the workplace.

Personal appearance is only important when others control your professional fate. If you build a company from the ground up, therefore, your success or failure depends little, if any, upon how you look. Of course, if you are a total slob, it might turn off potential customers to a degree. Even then, owners often hire others as their managers or "front men or women," according to Schmitt. But for the most part, business owners come in all shapes, sizes, and demeanors. If, therefore, you are "appearance challenged," you should give serious consideration to running your own show. Your odds of achieving major success may be higher on your own than they would be in a big organization.

Control What You Can

For those of us whose careers involve working our way up some-one else's organization, personal appearance will, therefore, always be an important factor in how far we go. There are several ways that you can improve the perception others have of your personal appearance. First, "Dress up just one step," says Hinshaw of Gray-bar. Casual days and casual attire in many office environments give those people who are "less good-looking" a real opportunity. Study your company's dress code and come to work dressed a notch above that which is required. If the company allows collared T-shirts, wear button-downs. If the company allows khaki pants, wear a set of nicely tailored dress slacks. For women, just a little extra attention to makeup or accessories or a little more neatly groomed hair styling over the norm can make you stand out from the crowd.

But do not overdo it. One female executive told me the story of a male subordinate who came to work, in a casual-dress office envi-ronment, wearing a suit with suspenders, a bow tie, and a hand-kerchief folded neatly in the pocket of his white button-down shirt. "He looked like a circus clown," said the executive. His presump-tuous, eccentric appearance did not help his career, she noted. Or, as Doug Bain of Boeing put it, "There are still some people—espe-cially men—that you could describe as looking like some kind of a 'dandy'—they are just dressed too perfectly. It is a distraction. It's like, what are you trying to prove?" The objective is to look sharp, not strange or presumptuous. Strike that balance and you are a step ahead of everyone else.

Next, learn the basic rule of manners and etiquette. Business decision makers notice people who are rough around the edges, and these people simply do not get promoted. You need to know how to greet and introduce people properly, which fork gets used for what, and how to write a thank-you note. These seemingly little issues can make or break a career, according to several of the top professionals I interviewed. For example, publisher Earl Graves told me that he makes a point of taking his grandchildren to black-tie events by the time they are eight years old so they can learn how to conduct themselves properly in formal situations. It really gives them a leg up on the competition, according to Graves, who stated unabashedly that he considers etiquette very important when he evaluates whether to hire or promote someone.

Do Not Confuse Individuality with Stupidity

Everyone feels a need to express his or her own individuality. But there are a lot of ways to express your individuality without adverse professional ramifications. You should never risk your career advancement in the name of some bizarre form of personal self-expression.

The vast majority of top professionals do not like tattoos, nose rings, or purple hair. As Dave Ruf, CEO of Burns & McDonnell, put it, "If a guy comes in here with a ponytail and earrings, he starts in a hole with me." It is not worth risking your career over such superficial expressions of individuality. Think about it. Shouldn't individuality be about deeper characteristics than a piece of metal on your tongue? Never stand on principle over petty appearance issues at the workplace. If glittered blue hair is the only way you have to express yourself, then you are not making much of a personal statement anyway. Anyone can do that.

Save most of your individual expression for activities outside the workplace. I know lawyers who jam with their electric guitars at home at night. I am one of them. Mike Marks, one of Boeing's senior managers, is a true-believing biker—he hobnobs with the motorcycle crowd on the weekends and then sells F-15s to Korea during the week. In most circumstances, there are better times and better places to express your individuality than at the office.

If you want to put some personal imprimatur on the office, take those elements that separate you from others and turn them into a professional plus. One of my acquaintances is a successful woman lawyer who wears interesting jewelry from her extensive world travels—Nigeria, Tibet, Korea, etc. This jewelry enhances her professional image because it shows that she has seen a lot of cultures and that she exhibits curiosity about the world around her. I know a successful professional, Paul Weil, whose avocation is photography. He takes great pictures and has blown up several of them and put them in the office. What it tells his clients is that he has a keen eye for detail. Norma Clayton of Boeing always puts a little of her favorite soft blue color scheme in her office. "I like warmth, and blue is a very warm color," notes Clayton.

This type of personal expression is fine, and is often helpful to a professional image. In fact, Norma Clayton noted the importance of staying attuned to the personal and office appearance of others with whom you work. If, for example, you walk into someone's office and you see "animal figurines with inspirational expressions" around them, "don't tell that person that you are going hunting this weekend," Clayton quipped. You not only have to make your careful expressions of personality at the workplace, but you have to look around and see what others are saying about themselves as well.

Which brings us to another point. Personal appearance includes not only yourself and your clothes, but also your office. I conducted most of the interviews for this book in the offices of the interviewees. Every one of them had a neat, well-organized office. A disorganized office sends the wrong professional message—and it can cause a lot of professional headaches as well. Some people take pride in the piles of paper on their chairs and boxes of junk on their floors. But have you ever noticed that those people are never at the top of the organization chart? Keep your desk neat and your chairs free of papers.

I Wish I Had the Time to Work Out

The Honorable Patrick Murphy, a former marine who is now the presiding federal judge in the Southern District of Illinois, told me that it ticks him off when out of shape people claim that "they do not have time to work out." *Everyone has time to work out.* It is simply a question of priorities. Those people who claim that they are too busy are (1) deluding themselves with lame justifications for their laziness and (2) insulting those who do work out by implying that they—the ones who do work out—are not busy enough with their careers or somehow have it easier than those who "do not have time" to work out. The next time you are tempted to say that you do not have time to work out, think about how many hours you spend watching golf or Ozzie Osbourne on TV—lying there on the couch with a beer. You do have the time to keep in shape.

Earl Graves agrees. "It is easy to say that 'my laces hurt' so I won't exercise. But you have got to do it. You can find time. I remember one time when I had a full day of meetings getting up at 5:00 A.M. in the dark and freezing cold in Michigan and working out with the CEO of Northrop. I said, 'If a car hits us, they won't find us for four hours.' But we did it. Sometimes you say to yourself, this is nuts, but you just find a time to do it. And it actually becomes enjoyable."

President Bush works out every day. A couple of years ago, I met the chief justice of the Supreme Court of the United States, William Rehnquist, at a swimming pool in Washington, D.C. We discussed the benefits of swimming for several minutes after our respective workouts. He felt it was an important part of his day. If the president and the chief justice can find time to work out, *so can you*!

All invincible executives take care of their bodies. They organize their physical selves as well as they organize their departments, business deals, and offices. They realize that the benefits of a healthy body are immeasurable. Less time away from work; more stamina during times of crisis; a sharper, more professional mind and image. "Health equals energy," according to Ron Gafford, CEO of Austin Industries. And energy is an essential element of long-term professional success.

Convert the Negatives to Positives

There is one advantage to being short or not so attractive at the workplace—and you can convert it into a major career plus. People have lower expectations when they first meet you. On the flip side, I know many instances of good-looking silver-haired men who ran into major professional trouble when it became apparent that they could not measure up intellectually to their physical appearances. People have high expectations of good-looking people. They tend to have lower expectations of the small, bald guy. That creates an opportunity for those of us who are physically challenged.

If you do not have the ideal physical appearance, first take the steps described above to maximize what you do have. Dress right, and use your office as means to convey your organization, depth of thought, and interests. Then play on the fact that people meeting you for the first time will not be blown away by their first impression of you. Juanita Hinshaw, CFO of Graybar, recommends that executives who are at a disadvantage—particularly women— "listen and know when to speak. . . . You have to know that what you say is going to make an impact." Carefully plan when you will make your move to impress that customer, boss, or client. And then—only when the time is right—speak with well-organized confidence. Doug Bain of Boeing notes that a resonant voice "instantly connects with people and commands a certain respect." You can literally silence a room that way. I have seen it happen many times. In fact, a confident voice is most effective when it is attached to an average-looking person. People with less-than-ideal appearances need to make every word count, and when they do so, they develop a sort of corporate charisma such that everyone turns to listen when they talk. You can do it too.

RULE

18

Take the High Ground and Never Give It Up

 **SNAPSHOT**

Are ethics an essential element of long-term success?

Yes: 98 percent   **No:** 2 percent

Unsurprisingly, a supermajority of invincible executives say that ethical conduct is a critical element of their success. They *have to say it*. But do they really believe that the good guy finishes first? The answer is no. Everyone with whom I discussed the issue agreed that unscrupulous people can go very far in the business world.

But, in order to achieve "invincible" status, you must remain ethical. The reason is simple: as soon as you cross the line into unethical territory, even for just a moment, you are forever vulnerable to a career-ending turn of events. This vulnerability can manifest itself in terms of criminal liability, bad press, or a reputation-damaging lawsuit—you never know until it hits. By definition, therefore, you lose your invincibility the moment you cross the ethical line.

Those who conduct themselves unethically may reach dizzying levels of success, but they will always be looking over their shoulders. That paranoia manifests itself in the way they treat customers, clients, and coworkers. It hurts their careers even if the wrongdoing is never exposed. By contrast, those who stay within the bounds of professional ethics feel no such vulnerability and can conduct their affairs with self-confidence.

Ethical Lapses Will Haunt You

About ten years ago, a man we will call Philip served on the board of directors of a major American company. At a board meeting, Philip learned that a company internal investigation had discovered that one of its employees in South America had probably paid off government officials of five countries in an attempt to get the company preference for government contracts. If true, this was a clear violation of United States laws. The employee had allegedly paid these officials over fifty thousand dollars. Upon learning of the bribery, the board voted to fire the employee, as well as seven others who reportedly knew about the practice but did not report it. However, company counsel concluded—correctly under the particular circumstances of the case—that there was no *legal* requirement that the company make any affirmative disclosure of the bribery—either to the public or to law enforcement officials in the United States. In fact, it did not appear that the alleged bribery had even gotten the company the contracts in question.

Philip thought that the company should "come clean" as a matter of pure ethics and make a disclosure to federal officials anyway. However, Philip could not convince the other board members to do so. His proposed resolution to issue a press release and turn the evidence over to the government failed by a twelve-to-three vote. Philip resigned from the board but felt he could not make a unilateral disclosure in violation of the board vote, especially since the board's position was legally defensible.

"So now," Philip said, "I just sit here waiting for the day that a witness or one of the disgruntled fired employees goes public, and the world finds out that I knew about it and said nothing. I'll be living with this every day. Today could be the day my reputation is ruined. Or maybe tomorrow. Or maybe the next day . . ."

That is what happens when you have to live with an unethical act—or even a failure to act, as occurred in Philip's case. It haunts you every day.

Can You Learn Ethics?

Clyde Tuggle, who is vice president in charge of worldwide communications at Coca-Cola, always makes his points succinctly. He notes that "you cannot teach someone to be ethical. Either you are ethical or you are not." Other top executives with whom I have discussed the issue agree. For example, top banker Drew Baur practically echoed Mr. Tuggle's statements when he told me that "you can't put an adjective in front of the word 'honest.' Either you are or you are not." You have to decide on your own whether you are going to conduct yourself ethically. No one can make you do it.

Unfortunately, however, merely deciding to be ethical does not make you ethically invincible. Ethical people often find themselves in trouble because they did not understand or know where the ethical line was, or because they received bad advice regarding what was proper and what was improper. In certain areas of business, such as exporting, environmental law, taxation, and doing business with the government, the standard of ethical conduct is often counterintuitive.

Moreover, many senior executives get into trouble because they failed to communicate the proper ethical standard to others or because they hired people who did not have the same commitment to ethics that they did. As you get higher in a professional structure, there will be an increasingly greater number of people whose conduct will be imputed to you. That presents a huge risk to your career.

Five Rules of Professional Ethics

In order to weather their ever-increasing ethical responsibilities, invincible executives with whom I have spoken (or whom I have studied) identify up to five key strategies that keep them away from ethical scandals.

1. **Recognize that standards of professional ethics have become increasingly stringent over the past decades.** You cannot use the ethical standards of your mentors and predecessors as guideposts for your own conduct. You can no longer get away with conduct that was once accepted and commonplace on the job—be it an office romance with a subordinate or an aggressive campaign to trash the competition.

Ed Dowd, a former U.S. attorney and currently a leading white-collar criminal defense lawyer—as well as an amateur historian—notes that virtually all of the competitive tactics used by tycoons like the Rockefellers and the Carnegies in the late nineteenth and early twentieth centuries would be illegal now. The tycoons of the Industrial Revolution conspired to monopolize their industries, exploited inside information for their personal gain, and obtained a stranglehold on the U.S. financial system. These tactics were legal when they did them, and the tycoons considered such actions to be good, aggressive business. What was tough business yesterday is bad business today.

Fast-forward almost a century. Microsoft, Enron, and Merrill Lynch executives have been caught in serious ethical and legal scandals for engaging in similar business tactics. They have respectively been accused of conspiring to damage competitors, inventing clever legal structures to manipulate their financial status, and giving advice without disclosing conflicts of interest. As a result, they have suffered bad damage to their images, with the majority of Americans considering them to be unethical companies. New age, new standards.

Similarly, the civil rights laws, environmental laws, export control laws, government contracting laws, and corporate fraud laws passed from 1960 to 2002 make all kinds of conduct illegal that was not only legal before then but ethically acceptable as well. "There is no excuse for operating a business in the year 2003 as if it were 1903, 1963, 1993, or even last year. Standards change and executives have to learn the new rules," says Dowd.

There remains a tendency of executives whose careers are on the rise to become dizzy with their success and to believe that they can get away with more now than they once could. The fact is that law and ethics hold more powerful people to a higher standard than they do less powerful people, and the standards get tighter every day. Do not fall into the "tycoon mind-set" or you risk a huge fall.

2. Win against unethical foes by finding the most ethical route and promoting it aggressively and uncompromisingly. While it is important to be the "good guy," you do not have to be the "nice guy."

A mid-level management consultant related a story to me that illustrates the point perfectly. He was at a meeting in which executives of a midsized construction company briefed their CEO on a problem between the construction company and a major steel products supplier. The steel supplier felt that the construction company had misrepresented the scope of work for a particular job and wanted more money to complete the job.

The construction company executives informed the CEO that his company had indeed expanded the scope of work. They noted that not only was the steel supplier entitled to more money, but the supplier had also conscientiously continued to perform—spending its own money pending the receipt of additional funds from the construction company. Finally, the CFO told the CEO that the supplier would likely go bankrupt without the additional money that was due to it.

The CEO asked the CFO what his options were. The CFO said, "Your only ethical options are to (a) terminate the supplier in accordance with the terms of the contract, pay his costs, pay profit on those costs, and hire another steel supplier to complete the job; or (b) modify the existing contract to reflect the increased scope of work, and pay our current supplier more money—he is entitled to it."

The CEO—known for his cutthroat tactics—looked the CFO in the eyes and asked her, "What are my unethical options?"

"What?" asked the CFO.

"You said I had two *ethical* options. I want to know *all of my options.*"

"Well," she said, "it was just a phrase. I can't think of any other options."

Just then, a young protégé of the CEO chimed in smarmily. "I can think of two other options," he said. "First, you could sue them, seeking an order that they continue to perform. They could not afford to fight us and would declare bankruptcy within a week. We could pick them up cheap in bankruptcy court. Second, you could offer to renegotiate the contract, give them just enough extra cash to keep them afloat, but do so only on the condition that they not enter into future contracts with our competitors—so at least we could gain some tactical advantage by giving them the money we owe them."

The CEO looked at the CFO and said, "That is the kind of thinking I like." Ultimately, for reasons of legal and schedule risk rather than ethics, the CEO chose to modify the contract without extracting the suggested concessions. But the lesson of the conversation was clear. Unethical people always have more options than ethical people do.

There is only one way to gain a tactical advantage over a person like this CEO—a person who has more options because he or she is not bound by any sense of ethics: pick one option—the most ethical one—and present it as the only option. "You seize the high ground and never give it up," says former Senator John Danforth. That means you determine the most ethical path, you make it clear to those who want to follow a lesser path that there will be negative ramifications to their proposed course of conduct, and you refuse to compromise.

When it comes to seizing the high ground, Senator Danforth practices what he preaches. When he became the Waco Special Counsel, he gathered his staff together and told them the following: "All of the independent counsel investigations from Iran-Contra to Ken Starr were marred by covert leaks to the press—a questionable tactic that hurt the rights of those being investigated and marred the credibility of the investigators. Our rule is no leaks. Not one person says one thing to one member of the press until after we are done. One strike and you are out."

Senator Danforth found the high ground in the battle of the leaks and laid down the law. The result was, for the first time ever in a major federal investigation, there were no leaks—not one during the entire fourteen months of his investigation. Neither he nor his staff responded even when patently false statements about his investigation appeared in the press. No compromises. Danforth's no-leak approach even earned the grudging respect of the media. There were articles marveling at how quiet everyone kept during his investigation. Seize the high ground and you may suffer some criticism, but, as long as you refuse to compromise, you will prevail.

3. Learn the technical or legal limits on your professional conduct. As I mentioned earlier, a lot of businesspeople feel that legal and technical issues gum up the smooth operation of an organization. Recently, a very senior aerospace executive, Stephanie, shared with me on condition of anonymity an e-mail from the CEO of another aerospace executive. The two companies were joint venturers on a major defense contract. Stephanie had requested a thorough legal review of some information that the joint venturers were sending to the government customer as a contract "data deliverable." Her counterpart sent her an e-mail to the following effect: "Stephanie. Why are you mucking up our deal with a bunch of legal crap? We are supposed to be senior executives, here. We know how to do a deal and all the lawyers do is try to take things over and shut things down. What are you made of?"

This man will never be an invincible executive. In fact, his company is teetering on the edge of financial disaster as I write this chapter—in large part due to staggering legal payouts from mistakes made by his "hard-charging" executives, who routinely ignore or circumvent the company legal staff.

There are many situations where law runs contrary to intuition. Consequently, you need to have constant coaching on where the legal lines are. The result of failing to do so is finding yourself accused of unethical conduct even when your intentions were good. Here are some examples:

• *Contracting with the government.* In the commercial world, you guard with your life information that goes into pricing your goods or services. You never let anyone know what your product really costs you. In many government procurements, however, you are legally obligated to disclose all information that goes into setting your price—including your confidential cost data. There are literally hundreds of people who have served time in prison and thousands more whose careers were ruined when they kept relevant pricing information from the government because disclosing it simply ran contrary to the way that they were used to doing business in the commercial world. Good legal advice would have avoided these career catastrophes.

• *Exporting.* Joe Hepworth, a Boeing lawyer and a man of tremendous integrity, tells the story of a an executive who hurt her career a few years ago when she gave a PowerPoint presentation to a potential customer in a foreign country. She did not know that the viewgraphs she had stored on her computer and taken overseas constituted the "exporting of technical data" under the Arms Export Control Act. By failing to get an export license for her presentation, she had literally committed a federal exporting violation.

• *Sexual harassment.* Many people think that harassment involves directing offensive conduct at a particular individual. Supreme Court cases, however, have established that even a few dirty jokes, not directed at anyone in particular, can create a "hostile work environment" to all women, giving them all a lawsuit against your company.

Invincible executives do not engage in relationships with subordinate coworkers. That is an obvious one. But they go much further. They do not make sexually explicit jokes on the job; they do not view sexually explicit material on the job; and they do not turn a blind eye to subordinates who do these things. Rather, they respond decisively and forcefully against e-mails, comments, or innuendos on the job that female workers might find offensive. Keep in mind, also, that federal civil rights violations can occur when women harass men and in situations of same-sex harassment as well.

• *Environmental law.* You may be responsible for cleaning up chemicals that you did not even put on your premises. You can in rare circumstances even be liable for not doing anything about a toxic chemical problem that you did not cause. Prosecutors in environmental cases have tremendous power and can put your company through hell even for what might seem to you to be minor infractions. Never consider an environmental issue to be too minor to warrant your full attention.

• *Antitrust and unfair competition.* The rules on what you can do to trash the competition are becoming increasingly tough. Chances are that the moment you turn your attention away from making your product the best and start trying to bring down the competition, you are running afoul of some federal or state law that protects competition.

• *Insider trading.* You no doubt read about Martha Stewart and the mega-rich ImClone executives and allegations of their insider trading. Do not be fooled into thinking that insider trading is a problem reserved for the rich and famous. The biggest insider trading scandal of the past several years occurred at IBM when a secretary passed on confidential information to her husband, who in turn passed it on to a teacher, pizza parlor owner, doctor, and several others. They all made a few thousand dollars and were all indicted for insider trading. There is no such thing as someone "too small or too remote" to be nabbed for insider trading.

As the examples above indicate—and they are just a few of many counterintuitive areas of the law—a lot of well-meaning people find that their careers end because they did not understand where the ethical line was. While ethics goes far beyond technical legality, it is important for every top executive to remain well-briefed on significant changes in ethical standards that might affect his or her conduct, and it is important that top executives let people at all levels know that they expect all executives in the organization to remain well-advised of legal standards. Everyone from Sheryl Crow, the singer, to Pat Finneran, former marine, recognizes and emphasizes the importance of sound professional guidance to long-term success. They flatly reject the "lawyers will mess things up" attitude that has ruined so many careers.

4. Remember that ethical standards are subjective. "In 95 percent of the cases where you accuse someone of being unethical, they legitimately believe that you are the unethical one," an Anheuser-Busch executive once told me. That is because there are legitimate different interpretations of the ethical line. You need always to anticipate what others will say about your conduct, not only what you yourself think about it. Then, be well prepared to counter their claims

Where possible, act in a manner that even your foes cannot turn against you. For example, while the law establishes that a single dirty joke probably does not create a "hostile work environment" under civil rights laws, it is unclear just how many jokes will take you across the line. The truly ethical person, therefore, tells no such jokes. That is always safe; that is always ethical.

And never think that an ethical transgression is too trivial to be of significance. Jim DeVita, the New York assistant U.S. attorney who prosecuted New York hotel queen Leona Helmsley for tax fraud, told me that Ms. Helmsley kept saying that she could not be a tax cheat because she paid hundreds of millions in taxes and was only accused of withholding about $1.2 million. To her, a mere $1.2 million may have been trivial. Others saw the situation a little differently. Companies have fired employees for overstating expense accounts by twenty-five dollars. Do not decide that your ethical transgression may be too minor to be a problem. The decision maker may disagree.

5. Convey the ethics message to those who work for you in a substantive, repetitive manner that neither trivializes nor commercializes ethics. Companies from Silicon Valley to Wall Street plaster "Ethics First" or some variation of that slogan in their cafeterias and hallways and in their company newsletters. They spend millions of dollars on T-shirts, coffee mugs, and Post-its that proclaim the importance of organizational ethics. A couple of years ago, a financial service executive showed me some of his ethics trinkets, stating sarcastically, "We do not have a *culture* of ethics, we have a *cult* of ethics." Even his key chain had an ethics slogan on it. The next year, however, this man's company paid a fine in excess of $50 million to the government for fraudulent sales practices.

In a similar vein, I recently toured a United States military facility and saw a poster on the walls that emphasized the importance of ethical conduct. Less than two months later, a squadron commander who worked at the facility was court-martialed for directing subordinates to falsify aircraft maintenance records.

Consistently, my research reveals that the vast majority of large companies that have been convicted of white-collar criminal acts over the past ten years had highly touted codes of ethics. Merrill Lynch, which had frequently proclaimed its commitment to ethics, paid $100 million to settle charges of conflicts of interest. Both Arthur Andersen and Enron had codes of ethics.

Too often companies pay only superficial deference to ethics— lots of glitz and no substance—or they devote a lot of time and money to developing real ethics policies and then fail to communicate them to the employees—the policies just sit on a shelf gathering dust. Invincible executives recognize that the unethical acts of their subordinates will be imputed to them, so they take ethics training very seriously.

Ethics Training

There are three elements to effective ethics training. First, the organization must develop substantive, comprehensive rules of conduct. Second, executives must communicate those rules in a readily understandable and repetitious manner. Providing a dense set of manuals is as bad as trivializing ethics with coffee mugs. Invincible executives skip the trinkets and supplement the paperwork with accessible, interesting online training, as well as in-person seminars delivered in a dynamic and engaging way. If employees read about ethics in a manual, take an online course, and then attend a seminar that focuses on real-life cases, the message will come across loud and clear.

Finally, invincible executives insist on monitoring success, according to Walter Metcalfe, chairman of Bryan Cave, one of the country's largest international law firms. They have employees take tests that show they understand their ethical obligations, and they monitor "ethics trends" within their organizations—i.e., how many transgressions occurred in a given period of time and the remedial actions taken.

Stick to Your Ethics—Always

As you strive to maintain an ethical standard of conduct, remember that part of being ethical is being consistent. Unethical people, according to publisher Earl Graves, tend to shade a situation for a particular audience—altering or changing their story or their spin on it. If you adopt that approach, you will eventually get caught and your career will flame out. Graves puts it this way: "You can wake me up in the middle of the night, and what you heard this afternoon is what you are going to hear tonight. I am not going to feed you bull. I don't have to remember the second time what I told you the first time because it is going to be the same. You can put that in your book." That is the essence of true professional ethics

A strange note on the ethics of the invincible executive. It seems that top professionals can get away with a lot more in their personal lives than they can in their professional lives. Charismatic leaders ranging from former President Clinton to Rudolph Guiliani, to Jack Welch and the CEOs of several Fortune 500 companies, have survived professionally despite past drug use, extramarital affairs, and the like. While holding your standards of personal conduct to the same level as your standard of professional conduct is very desirable, it quite frankly—and bizarrely—does not seem to be an absolute prerequisite to long-term success. Most invincible executives respect the privacy of others because they expect others to do the same for them. They tolerate personal transgressions—especially those in the distant past—as long as the actions in question have not impacted professional performance or created a legal risk at the office.

In fact, those who try to impose personal moral standards in a professional context are often the most vulnerable to attack. Who can forget the hypocrisy of former House Speaker Newt Gingrich when he criticized President Clinton's personal morals, all the while having an affair with a staffer? Invincible executives seem to be exceedingly careful not to criticize the personal lives of others. If they do and are clean themselves, they look like moralistic do-gooders; if they criticize others while hiding their own transgressions, they are setting themselves up for a catastrophic fall.

RULE
19

Don't Lose Your Confidence for Very Long

📷 **SNAPSHOT**

Have you ever felt burned out or otherwise lacking in confidence?

Yes: 40 percent   **No:** 60 percent

Invincible executives do not wring their hands, and they do not run out of steam. Janet Reno told me that, despite her health problems, she has never felt burned out or unable to do her job. In fact, less than half of the people with whom I have discussed the issue experienced what they would term "burnout." And those who do, regain their confidence quickly.

Avoid Energy-Draining Hand-Wringing

One major cause of burnout is dwelling on past problems and thinking about what "could have been" in your career. "It is a totally unproductive exercise that drains your energy," says aerospace consultant Tom Gunn. Invincible executives assimilate past mistakes and use them as guideposts to chart a future course, but they do not spend a lot of time regretting their mistakes or thinking what could have been. "Forgive yourself" for your past failures and move on, says former Senator Alan Simpson.

Because they do not dwell on the past, top professionals are not as likely as others to experience burnout. As Roger Kennedy, former head of the Smithsonian Institution, put it, "Top people study history, but they do not dwell on it." And if you are going to reflect on the past, Bill Shaw of Marriott notes, "reflect on the successes that you have had, not the failures."

People feel burned out because they are not happy with the results of their hard work. If you are looking forward most of the time, therefore, burnout rarely becomes an issue.

Stay Physically Strong

Enough about the philosophy of burnout. Let's talk about the physics of it. Top executives do not tire easily. They have tremendous endurance and boundless energy. According to Admiral Prueher, they have to have a "surge capability"—the capacity to increase their already high energy levels when crisis situations present themselves. As I said earlier, most of them work out and keep in good shape. "An hour workout gives me two hours of extra work capability," says Judge Murphy, whom we met earlier. It is an essential investment that you must make a minimum of three and preferably five times a week.

Working out does more than make your body strong. It cleans out your mind as well. "When I am having trouble writing a brief, I go for a swim," a successful Washington, D.C., lawyer told me one day at the University Club swimming pool. "In the pool, there is total sensory deprivation. No cell phones. No chattering in the halls. It is amazing how my mind replenishes itself as the water swirls around me. When I get back to the office, the brief practically writes itself. Everything has fallen into place."

One of the most senior people I interviewed for this book confided to me that, after a medical checkup revealed some heart problems, he hired a "stress coach" who helped him immeasurably in keeping his stress levels under control. That is a recurrent theme in my study of executives with staying power. Top people do not feel that they can do it alone. They are eager to seek help in any area when they need it, and they are not too proud to say that they need help.

As we touched on earlier, most successful executives also make a specific and conscious effort to carve out family and hobby time to help them stay grounded. Ron Gafford, CEO of Austin Industries, actually schedules time with his family in the same way he might schedule a business meeting; of course, far more flexibility is built into the family schedule. And, as I mentioned before, a lot of top professionals do not need much sleep—two and a half hours a night for Mike Sears of Boeing. A few supplement short nighttime sleep hours with fifteen- or twenty-minute power naps during the day. As I mentioned earlier, Albert Einstein is supposed to have staggered his sleep in small increments throughout the day. He did pretty well for himself.

If you can alter your sleep patterns to squeeze a couple of extra hours out of the day, you will have a tremendous advantage over others with whom you are competing for promotions and recognition. Getting by on less sleep by staggering your sleep, taking naps, etc., can provide such a professional edge that it is worth experimenting a little with alternative sleep patterns to see if they can work for you.

Substance Abuse

A good number of invincible executives—despite their forward-looking attitude, family time, less need for sleep, and good work-out habits—do experience burnout. What causes it and how do they handle it?

One major cause of career burnout is substance abuse. Some of our most prominent politicians and jurists have admitted to substance abuse issues in their lives. There have been reports that President Bush had an alcohol problem when he was a young adult. Chief Justice Rehnquist developed a problem with prescription painkillers after years of excruciating back pain. Three people I interviewed for the book confidentially confessed to having burned out due to a substance abuse problem—alcohol in two cases, drugs in the other.

If a president, chief justice, and multiple top executives can succumb to substance abuse, so can you. Never delude yourself into thinking that you are too strong or successful to become dependent on a chemical. In fact, my informal research reveals that substance abuse tends to strike intelligent, creative, and charismatic people at least as often as it strikes those who are down and out. The greatest enemy to defeating a substance abuse problem is self-delusion.

"At first the drugs actually energized me, but it was like a snowballing mortgage on my life. For every couple of hours of extra lift I could get immediately, I needed a full day or more of recovery time," one of my interviewees told me. The other, an admitted alcoholic, said he began drinking to overcome shyness in social situations. "As I started to gain professional success, I was expected to do more socializing—at home, after work, at fund-raisers—and I found that a few drinks made the conversation easier."

In each case, it took about a year for the problem to manifest itself in the traditional ways—interfering with work and family life. And in each case, the invincible executive (1) admitted the problem outright; (2) sought help—from friends, family, and/or professionals; (3) went "cold turkey" and never looked back; and (4) as part of his own therapy, committed some time to helping others who had similar problems.

Another major cause of burnout is weathering a professional storm. I spoke earlier about how Sheryl Crow had to deal with biting statements from band members and coworkers after the success of her first CD. That left her feeling burned out. I also spoke about how aerospace executive Tom Gunn had to weather a two-year federal investigation into bribery that ultimately led to his exoneration.

Despite the differences in their professions, both Crow and Gunn handled the burnout associated with unfair accusations in a similar manner. Both opted for a change in scenery. Crow went from Los Angeles to her Missouri home and on to Europe; Gunn moved from St. Louis to Phoenix. A change in physical location—even if just for a couple of weeks—really helps you overcome burnout and other similarly stressful situations. Both did a lot of reading, as well. Crow read *The Fountainhead*, for example. Immersing yourself in another world—one where there is suffering and renewal—is also a critical element of overcoming burnout. Finally, every executive who admitted to burnout looked inward for guidance. Even those who were not previously religious added a spiritual dimension to their lives during times of crisis.

Dealing with Success

Some top executives feel the most vulnerable and burned out when they should be feeling great about themselves. Tom O'Neill, CEO of Parsons Brinckerhoff, noted that many people who enjoy great professional success experience a strange feeling of guilt—as if they did not really deserve to get to the level that they have achieved. "You think that you are going to get found out, that you are not as good as people think you are, and that you are not supposed to be here. That is a personality trait with a lot of us."

In fact, success has a backlash, and that backlash, unless recognized and dealt with, can cause top people to fall. Television executive producer Chris Lloyd told me that he experienced a very rough period after his sitcom "Frasier" won its fifth Emmy in a row. "I always thought, wow, wouldn't it be great to win an Emmy? And then I thought, well my dad won two Emmys, so wouldn't it be great to win two? And then I wanted to exceed my dad, so I wanted three. Suddenly we'd won three years in a row and I started thinking, well, you know the record for any series is four in a row. And suddenly you've won four and then, if we do it again next year, we'll set the all-time record. Which we did! And then, I showed up for work at the beginning of the sixth season, and I started thinking, I don't know what my next goal is here. And it became really tough." He felt that all he could do was go down, and that feeling created self-doubt. It was at that time that he decided to switch tracks and start developing new sitcoms. "Once you are at the top, all you can do is fall off. So it is better to climb a different mountain," Lloyd concluded.

While it might be comforting to know that even the most successful among us experience doubt, keep in mind that this doubt cannot last long if you want your career to remain invincible. Those who feel guilty about achieving success shrug those feelings off before they become a self-fulfilling prophecy. Those who feel that they have reached the pinnacle of success in one job quickly switch tracks to pursue new opportunities. You must do the same.

You Can and Must Develop Professional Charisma

📷 SNAPSHOT

What is the most important personality characteristic of an invincible executive?

Leadership: 21 percent
Drive/energy: 18 percent
Writing/speaking skills: 16 percent
Persistence: 11 percent
Intelligence: 9 percent
Self-confidence: 8 percent
Ethics: 7 percent
Other: 10 percent

There are several adjectives or phrases that invincible executives repeatedly use to describe people like themselves. For an outside perspective, I also asked a couple of executive recruiters what they look for in senior managers, and they too tended to rely upon a similar set of adjectives to describe the intangible qualities of invincible executives.

"The bottom line here is that you have to *shine*," an executive recruiter told me. Shining means being a "continuous source of light—through perseverance, humor, depth, ethics, and confidence." Another headhunter said, "The really great professionals have a certain *veneer* of success." It comes across in the way they look, the way they greet someone new, the way they analyze the facts and develop a strategy to resolve a business dilemma, and the humanity with which they accomplish some pretty result-oriented business objectives. "All of it emanates from self-confidence," she added.

Another word frequently used to describe the people who make it to the top is *magnetism*. People have to "gravitate to you like the Pied Piper," according to Richard Bell of HDR, Inc. They have to want to be around you.

Joe Ryan, the almost philosophical executive vice president of Marriott, says that true leaders have "velocity." He defines velocity as a combination of natural skill, ambition, and productivity. These factors blend together to create the most important feature of a leader: effective judgment. Good judgment in turn inspires confidence in those around you, and that confidence leads to an upward career path, according to Ryan.

Invincible executives also tend to make strong first impressions. Senator Danforth, for example, described President Bush by saying, "He shows you instantly that he is on top of the entire situation. He is tremendously impressive—immediately." Interestingly, I have heard many people say that they almost swooned in the presence of the senator as well. He too is legendary for the positive first impression that he makes on everyone.

Perhaps the most common phrase used by top professionals and executive recruiters to describe their type is *charisma*—the kind of professional personality that makes good people want to rally around you. Many people will tell you that charisma is an intangible quality and an inherent quality—i.e., you cannot measure it, and you cannot develop it. Based upon my interviews and studies, I disagree entirely. While there are certainly some people who have a natural presence about them, the majority of executives with staying power do not fall into that category.

As we discussed earlier, many invincible executives were painfully shy when they were younger. Many were socially disadvantaged and had a near–inferiority complex when they went out into the world—full of people with better educations and more affluent family backgrounds. Therefore, you can in fact *develop* that "veneer" of invincibility, that "charisma" that draws others to you. While the comments I received on this topic were rather diffuse, they came down to six basic ways that people develop a charismatic professional personality.

1. **Find out what you are good at and work tirelessly to be the best.** Finding and developing your talent was a theme early in the book. Charisma develops best when a person—especially one initially lacking in confidence or direction—finally finds his or her gift. Realizing that you excel in some professional skill is like a jolt of energy that can propel you forward for decades. It gives you direction and it provides you with self-confidence and self-satisfaction that transfers to others.

2. **Never shy away from a leadership role.** Over one-fifth of invincible executives believe that leadership is the number one characteristic that leads to professional success. That means you can never shy away from a chance to lead. Take on unpopular projects. Agree to be the lead person in dealing with difficult customers and suppliers. Remember, however, when you jump into difficult situations, keep expectations reasonable (or even perhaps a little on the low side) and then exceed them by leaps and bounds!

Exceeding expectations in difficult leadership roles gives you a "legendary" aura that creates professional charisma. You want to be the one about whom others say, "She's the person who landed the Jones project against impossible odds," or "He's the guy who took it to those government regulators and saved us five million bucks." Build a leadership track record by setting modest expectations— all the while having a plan to pull off a real coup. Then watch your professional reputation grow around you.

3. Work longer and with greater intensity than everyone else. High productivity sends ripples up an organization. Keep your desk and files organized, develop work-positive sleeping and exercise habits, and ensure that your family understands your priorities and you will begin to develop professional charisma among the decision makers in your career. Make it a habit to be on time for meetings and ahead of schedule in getting draft memos and presentations to superiors. Pick up your own phone when you are in the office— never force important superiors and customers to wade through assistants when you are in the office. It incenses them and is a very ineffective way of looking important.

4. Continuously develop communication skills and learn to draw information out of people. You have to write well, but your speaking ability is even more important than your writing skills, according to Bill Marriott. Most invincible executives have had professional assistance to improve their communication skills. If you cannot get professional experience, use volunteer activities, school board meetings, and other opportunities you have to give oral presentations to improve your communication skills. You have to be able to run a meeting and deliver a presentation with confidence, effective intonation, humor, and ease. "How you articulate an idea is as important as the idea itself," according to Admiral Prueher—

who demonstrated his communication skills on an international level when he served as U.S. ambassador to China during the tense standoff between the United States and China after a Chinese fighter plane collided with an American surveillance aircraft in 2001.

Perhaps the most critical part of charismatic communication is getting people to open up to you. People want to talk to charismatic leaders; they want to be around them. According to Ron Gafford, CEO of Austin Industries, a charismatic corporate leader "must be willing to share his or her life's experiences. Charisma also includes sharing your failures and the lessons learned from failures. Daring to be vulnerable is a part of charisma." And, Gafford adds, you use your open approach to communication to get others to open up to you to the point where you can draw out of them everything you need to know to run your business effectively. "Orchestrate the conversation so that others share at least as much with you as you have shared with them," Gafford says.

5. Develop the tough/tender reputation. You must be almost ruthless in your desire to improve your organization—financially, in terms of the quality of your product, and in terms of the reputation of your organization. Never take your eye off the fact that the principal goal of most organizations is to make money. (If it's a charity, the goal is to *raise* money.) That means anything you can do to increase profit margins should be a top priority. Coaching the company softball team, organizing the picnic, volunteering for the office beautification committee—to name a few examples I have seen on résumés—are all well and good, but they do not make money. You should focus more on product improvement initiatives, customer relations efforts, "tiger team" reviews of other parts of the organization, and similar such activities designed to add to the bottom line of the company.

But, at the same time, show a softer side during otherwise inconsequential moments. Take time to get to know the people working for you and for your bosses. Send them retirement and baby gifts; find something that they are interested in and talk about that when you see them in the hall or chitchat with them prior to a meeting. Show respect for their lives and career goals.

Finally, you have to be a cheerleader for your own people—encouraging them to improve their own professional standing by advancing the organization's interests. Praise should flow freely.

6. Know the facts cold. A young legal associate once made the interesting observation that "the higher up you get, the less people expect you to know about a particular situation." Invincible executives have an uncanny ability to be *underestimated* in this regard. They amaze people by the mere fact that they have done their homework. Being underestimated is good for a career. It has two components: first, not giving anyone a clue how much you really know, and second, springing it on everyone at the right time. Know how to play this important card well and all anyone will be saying after a meeting is, "Wow, that is one sharp person!" It is a key component to developing professional charisma. *Create situations like these where others talk about you so that you do not have to talk about yourself.*

PART

III

THE INVINCIBLE
MANAGEMENT STYLE

You have developed a reasoned, flexible route to success. You have the refined, charismatic personality that makes for long-term professional momentum. But if you cannot manage others well, you are anything but invincible. Professionally, you are dead in the water. It is time to supplement your career development and personality skills with an effective management style. Let's conclude the book with a discussion of how executives with staying power manage other people. How do they develop ever-increasing responsibility over ever-increasing numbers of people and projects while not losing control of the situation? How structured are their meetings? How do they resolve conflicts among employees? How do they get others to "buy in" to their plans?

You Can Only Micromanage Ten Employees and About Six Hundred Square Feet

◉ SNAPSHOT

Are you a micromanager?

Yes: 8 percent   **No:** 92 percent

You know what a micromanager is: someone who feels that he or she must control every aspect of the organization—from the color of the Post-its to the strategy for landing new customers.

There are a couple of simple truths about micromanagers. First, micromanagers tend to have very stable and relatively successful careers. They detect problems early. They know the details of their jobs so well that they are difficult to replace. Second, however, is the big downside. A marine colonel told me, "We do not promote our micromanagers. We love them right where they are." Bill Winter, chairman emeritus of Dr. Pepper/Seven Up, Inc., said almost exactly the same thing to me. What they meant by this statement is that there is a place for a micromanager, and it is squarely in the low to middle rungs of the organization. Bruno Schmitter of Hydromat agrees: "You need some micromanagers—in the right place." He adds that the right place is not at the top.

The colonel quoted above told me that he always has a micromanager running, for example, a supply room. "He or she will maintain tight control over everything that goes in and out of there; there will be no waste and no shenanigans. Perfect job for a micromanager." But you can be sure that this person will not be commanding the Third Army.

If your ambition is to have responsibility over a twenty-by-thirty-foot room full of supplies, micromanagement is the right style for you. It is very easy to build and maintain a *very small empire* through micromanagement. Many micromanagers can protect these little fiefdoms for decades, and they become downright proud of it. They can in fact become invincible in their very tiny domain.

The key to effective micromanagement is finding mindless people to work for you. As Richard Bell of HDR, Inc., put it, the only people who can work for a micromanager are "clones and robots." "You actually look for 'clock punchers' to work for a micromanager," the colonel referenced above told me. Anyone who really cares about or takes pride in his or her job will not want to work for a micromanager. But there are enough people out there who feel that a job is just a paycheck and who take pride in other areas of their lives that you can find a way to staff a micromanager's part of the organization, according to the colonel. The employees of a micromanager must be willing to do what they are told and not think much about it.

Mike Sears, executive vice president and CFO of Boeing, measures the domain of a micromanager not in terms of space but in terms of people. "How many people can you tell what to do every day?" he asks. "The number is between five and ten." But, he notes, the number of people you can *lead* is much, much greater. The human capacity for management simply does not allow you to micromanage more than a handful of other workers. Consequently, according to Sears, if you want to move to upper levels of management, you must become a leader and abandon micromanagement.

Juanita Hinshaw, CFO of Graybar Electric, provided a succinct explanation of why micromanagers never get too far: "Micromanagers are so busy doing someone else's job that they cannot focus on their own. For that reason they usually don't succeed in getting to the top."

So, yes, you can enjoy long-term professional success—on a very small scale—by micromanaging. But do you really want to look back on your career after you retire and say, "I was the best supply room manager the company ever had?" I hope not. Let's look for Plan B.

It's the People

It is essential to becoming an invincible executive that you learn to loosen the reins on your employees as you move up the management chain. During the early part of your career, you will be able to exert a fair amount of control over the people who work for you, if that is the way you prefer to manage. But you will become harried, frazzled, and resented if you try to micromanage greater numbers of people at higher levels in the organization.

It seems counterintuitive that as your responsibility increases, your willingness to give up control also has to increase. Invincible executives resolve this tension with three management tactics: (1) the ability to revert to micromanagement when a very specific problem arises, which we will cover in Rule 22; (2) developing excellent information flow, which we will cover in Rules 23 and 24; and (3) devoting a great deal of time to making sure that the right person is in the right job, which we will cover right now.

Invincible executives have the uncanny ability to pick the right person for the right job. In choosing the right person for a job, top professionals look not only at objective factors like competence, leadership, intelligence, and ethics, but also subjective factors like: Will this person work well with the person we currently have above him or her in the organization chart? Does this person have the personality type that will mesh with the particular clients or customers he or she is expected to deal with? Is the person well suited to the current and anticipated future projects of the organization?

Bill Shaw, president of Marriott International, notes that confident and competent managers do not micromanage because they do not want to make the organization totally dependent on them. "You need to let others develop the ability to run the show while you are gone," he says. For that reason, Shaw takes a very active role in "finding, developing, and retaining talent." Then he looks for opportunities and responsibilities to give away to his people—the antithesis of micromanagement.

From my interviews and research, I was surprised at how much time invincible executives spend choosing people rather than managing the organization. Recently, in connection with a legal matter, I had to review the e-mails sent between the CEOs of two companies that were in a joint venture on a major federal contract. The government customer was unhappy with the quality of the product. I would say that 90 percent of the e-mails between the two CEOs related to assessing the people who would be charged with fixing the quality problems, and only about 10 percent related to how the quality problems were actually going to be fixed. That is the way invincible executives avoid falling into the micromanagement trap—they focus on people who will resolve problems even more than the problems themselves.

Sports Authority

Great managers of sports teams seem to be very good at evaluating the subjective factors involved in picking the right person for the right job. They see not only the objective statistics that the player racks up, but also the subjective way that the individual will fit into the organization. That combination of evaluation skills is where the real synergistic benefits to the organization develop. For example, not too long ago, I heard Walt Jockety, general manager of the St. Louis Cardinals, talking to a group about baseball player Jim Edmonds. Jockety had traded a couple of decent but average players in order to get Edmonds. Everyone knew Edmonds could hit the ball, but he was underperforming in his current organization because the players and management of that organization did not mesh well with Edmonds's personality. The statistics alone would never have suggested that Edmonds could become an anchor player on a baseball team. However, Jockety thought Edmonds would do better under a low-key manager like Tony LaRussa in a city with fans who are not too hard on the players, like St. Louis. Sure enough, within weeks of his arrival in St. Louis, Edmonds was racking up numbers—in terms of both batting average and home runs—that far exceeded anything he had done for years at his old organization. And these numbers continued to be good years into the future.

This is just one example from my own hometown. Stories like this abound in the sports world among managers from Joe Torre of the New York Yankees to Scotty Bowman of the Detroit Redwings. They see more than the objective skills of a potential player. They understand which players will fit well into their organizations. That is what makes them invincible.

The Invincible Executive Delves into Specific Problems at Great Depth

📷 **SNAPSHOT**

Are you a "top level" manager?

Yes: 4 percent   **No:** 96 percent

Interestingly, while successful executives avoid being labeled micromanagers, they also do not consider themselves to be only "big picture" or "hands-off" managers. Bill Marriott, the CEO of Marriott International, says that some people confuse him with a micromanager, but in fact, he is not one at all. As a general rule, he picks good people and lets them do their jobs. However, invincible executives like Mr. Marriott cannot rely totally upon delegation—even to very reliable people. As we will discuss below, Mr. Marriott has a couple of exceptions to the delegation rule.

Sam Fox of the Harbour Group notes that a major flaw among some executives who do achieve success is a tendency to stop actively managing their business. They start to pay more attention to other interests and have a tendency to take their eye off the ball. According to Fox, if you are to enjoy long-term success, "You have to maintain a certain level of involvement in the details. I'm not advocating micromanaging. A good executive will know which of the details are significant and need to be understood."

Based on the interviews I conducted, there are four almost universally acknowledged guidelines for when to get into details.

1. Get input from all levels for major changes. Invincible executives often go two or three levels below their positions to solicit input when they are considering major corporate or organizational restructuring. They want to see the potential impact of a major organizational event from every perspective. So they will hold meetings with people at all levels of the organization and ask whether a proposed course of action will help or hurt their abilities to do their jobs.

At least ten people I interviewed described this sort of situation as one where they will in fact get into the details. For example, Ron Gafford, CEO of Austin Industries, firmly believes that micromanagement is a bad idea because it limits the span of leadership of the CEO, and it says "you don't trust your people." At the same time, Gafford feels it is essential to long-term success that managers, and especially senior managers, walk the company halls and floors to stay connected to the employees, greet them informally, and get input from all levels of the organization, especially when major changes are under consideration.

Janet Reno told me a story that illustrates this point when she set out to improve the operations of the United States Border Patrol. Rather than make decrees from on high, "I would go out to Border Patrol agents and ask again and again wherever I went, 'If you were the attorney general, what would you do to address the issues that are important to this country and to this department?' And they'd come up with great ideas. The women said, 'We need bulletproof vests that fit women.' I wasn't micromanaging. They knew I cared. The bulletproof vest issue was an example of how we must talk to the front line when we are looking to improve an organization. Interview the field, get their feedback, and then come up with policies."

2. Do spot checks. A significant minority of invincible executives believe that it is important to keep employees a little off guard, so that they do not become complacent about their jobs or their organizations. Admiral Prueher noted that you have to make occasional "spot checks" of your people at all levels. You take a "deep slice" from time to time, just to make sure that things are running smoothly at all levels. Similarly, Bill Marriott will occasionally pay a surprise visit to a distant site or a particular department in the organization. Word gets out that these types of visits are common and people remain committed to unwavering quality. Marriott notes that he has had to send many of his suits to the dry cleaners because he rubbed against hastily painted walls. Apparently, some of his hotel managers (who might, if they are lucky, get a few hours notice of his arrival) call the painters in at the last second. An occasional surprise visit or unexpected meeting will keep the people working for you on their toes.

3. Don't delegate a true crisis. Invincible executives abandon a delegation philosophy at the outset of an organizational crisis. While invincible executives tend to chart the general direction in good times, they manage crisis actively and aggressively as soon as the crisis is identified. Janet Reno had a "war room" during the Waco standoff, and many corporate executives have a similar "war management" mentality when their organization is confronted with a threat. That threat could be anything from an accounting scandal, to a lawsuit, to a project plagued with serious cost overruns.

In fact, most top executives who get fired, demoted, or fall from grace lose their invincibility for *failing to act quickly enough to address a growing crisis*. Often they deliberately distance themselves from a crisis on the mistaken belief that they can sidestep any adverse consequences by doing so. Bad idea.

Financial scandals in the past couple of years—from the Global Crossing and Adelphia scandals to the WorldCom debacle—have resulted in a tremendous skepticism of senior corporate management by the investing public. CEOs and other top executives have lost their jobs because of a public anger at managers who have allowed their company's financial situation to spin out of control without developing a quick action plan to address the problems. In many cases, it seems as if the managers were almost in a state of denial. In others, as apparently occurred with the ImClone insider trading scandal, the managers looked after their own personal interests but not the interests of their employees or average stockholders. All of the executives who followed the denial, self-interest, or self-distancing strategies saw their invincibility shattered.

Consequently, it is essential that when a crisis arises in your organization, you: (1) learn about it early; (2) acknowledge it—publicly if necessary to maintain integrity with your shareholders; and (3) aggressively manage the situation at the outset. Now eventually, if the crisis is a long-term one, you can return to more delegation. But at the outset, you have to be firmly in control, know every detail, and yes, micromanage the situation.

Military generals illustrate this point in an unusual but instructive way. For example, Lieutenant General John Sams, a former commanding officer of the U.S. Fifteenth Air Force, made the following observations and suggestions concerning micromanagement. He agrees that it is essential to show trust for those who work for you by giving them responsibility and letting them do their jobs. He does not condone micromanagement, even in times of war. General Sams believes, however, that there are occasional situations, most often during an unexpected, rapidly unfolding crisis, that a general officer must take a more hands-on and detail-oriented approach to management. However, because the military environment is so naturally hierarchical, General Sams emphasizes the seriousness of the situation by managing in a *less hierarchical* way when there is a crisis. "In those kind of situations, I tend to make myself part of the team. We sit around and brainstorm." He rolls up his sleeves and sits side by side with his subordinates to work on a resolution to the problem. Everyone has a voice—almost an equal voice until the final decision has to be made. General Sams does not micromanage by fiat or by spouting off orders. He micromanages by consensus. It has always worked very well for him, and it is a good lesson for those of us in the civilian world as well.

4. **Recognize the talents of all employees.** Executives with staying power recognize that their power derives from the work and intellect of their employees. If managers are to retain the support of their employees, they must communicate with them. Southwest Airlines CEO Jim Parker calls this concept "servant leadership," and it requires a "bypass structure" whereby senior managers communicate directly with junior managers on a regular basis.

"We fire people who lose the support of their people," according to Parker. Executives with staying power are pushed upward from below, Parker adds. In order to rise up the ranks, therefore, it is important that, no matter how high up in an organization you may rise, you retain the capacity and desire to speak with employees at all levels about their individual concerns and proposals for improving the company. This is not micromanagement, which tends to get everyone bogged down. Rather, it is an energizing process that allows managers to stay totally tuned in to the morale of their employees.

As they advance in their respective organizations, invincible executives loosen the reins on their subordinates—both out of management necessity and out of respect for the quality of their subordinates. But they never let go of the reins. And during times of crisis or when specific concerns regarding one part of the organization arise, they are able to resurrect their capacity to bore down into the details of a problem.

Intimidation Chases Away Talent, Opportunity, and Creativity

📷 SNAPSHOT

Do you manage by intimidation?

Yes: 4 percent   **No:** 96 percent

We discussed anger in Part II and found that it was a valuable tactic if used sparingly, carefully, in a controlled manner, and with a signature style. It follows, therefore, that management through intimidation—where the entire organization lives in permanent fear of a tyrannical boss or CEO—is not an effective management style—because it is not sparing, careful, controlled, or stylized.

Hold on! Some of the most successful corporate executives of all time ruled their organizations with an iron fist—starting with the prototypical tycoon, banker J. P. Morgan. Two of the people I studied for this book were described by former employees as executives who, respectively, implemented a "reign of terror" and "made top executives tremble." Both of these executives—who will remain nameless here—enjoyed tremendous professional success—winning awards and praise from the national media. One employee of one of these men told me the story of seeing this executive put his face about two inches away from the face of a senior subordinate who had failed to complete a project on time. The CEO yelled at this subordinate until the CEO's spit was rolling down the face of the subordinate. When the CEO was done, the subordinate, trembling, went into the bathroom and had to wash his face off. Outbursts like this were a common occurrence at this highly successful company.

So certainly you *can* succeed when you manage by intimidation. Many very successful people have done exactly that. But you have to play the odds—and here is why management by intimidation is not the right route for most people.

The Passing of T-Rex

Intimidation is an outdated management tool. Both of the intimidators to whom I referred are over sixty-five years old. While management by intimidation used to work pretty well, it rarely works today and can backfire big time. I had a very insightful conversation on exactly this topic with Richard Bell, the chairman and CEO of HDR, Inc.—a major employee-owned international building and construction group. He attributes the decline of the tyrannical dinosaurs to the advance of technology and the freedoms associated with technology. "In the 1980s you could get away with being a tyrant. But now this world is built on the Internet. There are more choices, and nobody has to be trapped anymore." Intimidation in today's business environment, according to Bell, chases away the talent and leaves people who are either desperate, sycophants, or vacuous.

Doug Bain of Boeing also believes that management by intimidation is on the way out. "The more temper you show, the less successful you will be," according to Bain. He attributes this change in the business climate to the rise of "individual rights" in the workplace over the past twenty-five years. Employees used to consider themselves as a tiny part of a big community. That meant they would tolerate intimidating managers. Now, with the advancement of workplace rights, individuals see themselves as having more power, and they will not put up with intimidators.

No Risk, No Reward

Intimidation limits opportunity. For any organization to be truly successful, the senior executives must learn of all opportunities, including those that involve significant risk. If you rule by intimidation, it eliminates calculated risk taking, because people fear incurring your wrath and will not present you with options that involve any risk of failure, according to Ron Gafford, CEO of the construction giant Austin Industries in Texas. "I have seen organizations where people were just so reticent to make a mistake that they refused to capitalize on opportunities," Gafford notes. Similarly, Sam Fox of the Harbour Group believes that "people will not take calculated risks" if they believe they will be severely criticized. Consequently, if you rule by intimidation, you are limiting the opportunities that you and your organization will have to make money.

You Stifle Yourself

Intimidation snuffs out creativity. Back when industrial manufacturing dominated the United States economy, companies were founded by a visionary genius and a few of his closest scientific or engineering peers. They had a lock on corporate creativity. Once the product went into the manufacturing phase, consistency and conformity were the most valued traits both in the product and in the workers who churned out hundreds and thousands of the product. The next Model T was supposed to be exactly like the previous one. The CEO did not want creativity—he (and it was a *he*) wanted efficiency, output, and uniformity. Tyrants are very good at getting that.

What they are not good at is getting innovation out of their employees. Today, with an increasingly service-oriented and decentralized workforce, creativity is now important at almost all levels of most organizations. In a tyrannical atmosphere no one dares to suggest anything out of the ordinary. Consequently, there is no product improvement, no increase in efficiency, and no adaptation to the changing strategies of competitors. That is why the management tyrants are going the way of the dinosaurs.

Bumpy Ride

Finally, as Dave Ruf, CEO of Burns & McDonnell, notes, people abandon a tyrant at the first sign of trouble. Leona Helmsley was the queen of New York when her hotel empire was intact, but when she found herself in trouble with the IRS, people were coming out of the woodwork to get even with her. A former maid Helmsley had fired testified that she had said, "Only the little people pay taxes." It was an out-of-context quote that had no direct bearing on the specific legal issue that got Ms. Helmsley incarcerated, but the alleged statement got swirling international press—mainly because it showed the depth of hatred people felt toward her.

More recently, Martha Stewart was implicated in an insider trading scheme. While I have never met Ms. Stewart, books and public reports indicate that there are a lot of people who consider her to be very autocratic, and quite bluntly, many people do not like her. Unsurprisingly, at the very beginning of the scandal—before there was any solid support for allegations that she engaged in insider trading—reports surfaced that many of her friends had dropped her like a hot potato.

Historic figures from Mussolini to Nixon illustrate the same point. Tyrants only have friends while they are in complete control. At the first sign of a crack in the tyrant's organizational structure, everyone abandons him or her. *Schadenfreude* is a German word for the sinful pleasure people take in seeing high-level people fall from grace. People take a lot more pleasure in seeing tyrants lose their thrones than they do those who have gained their prominence through respect for others.

24

Spend More Time on Information Inflow than Information Outflow

📷 **SNAPSHOT**

Do you think it is more important to get information than to give direction?

Yes: 75 percent   **No:** 25 percent

We discussed earlier the negative effect management intimidation has on both organizational opportunity and employee creativity. Intimidation also has a seriously negative effect on information flow. If people are scared of you, they do not want to bring you bad news. Moreover, they will filter or distort the truth if they fear your reaction to it. So if you manage by intimidation, you either get bad information or no information. As Doug Bain of Boeing puts it, "If somebody is going to get screamed at, that somebody is less likely to bring you bad news that you need to know. . . . Most managers deal with information flow. And personality plays a big role in whether information is getting to them and flowing within the organization."

Several invincible executives I interviewed said that accurate information flow is perhaps the most essential factor in long-term success. According to Bill Marriott, "As soon as people stop talking to you, you are dead." Similarly, Juanita Hinshaw, CFO of Graybar Electric, says that developing faithful reporting channels is the key to professional advancement. You have to be reasonable in your expectations, however. Her rule is: do not surprise me three times. "I tell people what I need and want and let them do it. I will leave you alone to do your job as long as you keep me posted, keep me informed. Let me know if there are problems or other issues that I need to deal with. . . . I don't want surprises. And one of the rules I am really hard on is that you do not surprise me three times," according to Hinshaw. One surprise she can understand; twice is a problem, but she is a forgiving person; three times and you are out of here. Hinshaw simply will not work with someone who repeatedly fails to get her accurate information in a timely manner.

Admiral Prueher noted that the higher up you get in an organization, the more prone your subordinates are to shading the facts of a situation to make them more palatable to you. "When you get to be a flag officer [an Admiral]," according to Admiral Prueher, "you never get another bad meal and you never get the truth," he told me. Consequently, "you always have to look carefully at what people are telling you, second-guess their motives, and find people whom you can rely upon."

Therefore, while invincible executives do not micromanage, they do spend a lot of time gathering information. In fact, they spend more time getting information than giving direction. To gather information effectively, they utilize three strategies: (1) they cultivate the personal management qualities that facilitate the flow of information to them; (2) they put people around them who are conduits for accurate information; and (3) they put organizational structures in place that permit the free flow of information.

Ask and Listen

First, executives with staying power know how to ask a question, and they know how to listen. Jim Parker of Southwest Airlines believes that "knowing how to ask a question is the most important skill you can have." He adds that you can never refrain from asking a question out of fear of sounding stupid. It is better to find out the answer now than make a mistake because you were too embarrassed to ask a question.

Then you have to listen to the answer. According to Ron Gafford, CEO of Austin Industries, one of the most important personal management qualities that ensures good information flow is the ability to listen effectively. In fact, a wide array of people I interviewed, from aerospace executive Tom Gunn to Congressman Richard Gephardt, emphasized the importance of retaining the ability to listen—no matter how successful you become. On the flip side, a common character flaw in executives who lose their professional invincibility is the need to dominate every conversation. Tom O'Neill, CEO of the engineering giant Parsons Brinckerhoff in New York, notes that when you start to have some success in the world, it becomes easy to think that you know more than everyone else. As a result you either stop listening to others entirely or you only listen to your little corps of confidants, and you lose touch with what is really going on with your company. "That kind of pride and hubris is deadly to a career," O'Neill notes.

Dr. Joshua Korzenik, the leading medical researcher we met earlier, notes that "as soon as you think you have it all together, you have ended your ability to innovate." Instead, you become "ossified" and you can no longer advance in your career and in your thinking. Invincible executives are always learning, and to learn you need to listen.

In fact, it is a common theme in my research that invincible executives assume that they know *less* than everyone else. Consequently, they do not interrupt or cut short those who are reporting to them on relevant topics; they do not put words in other people's mouths; and they do not finish other people's sentences. The truly invincible leader does not feel a need to assert his or her authority in every conversation. To do so cuts short the information flow process.

But Don't Listen to Everything

However, do not confuse the need to be a good listener with the need to listen to droning baloney. You only need to listen to *relevant information*. Part of your job as an executive who excels is to discern relevant information from irrelevant information. "Brilliant leaders spot issues better than others, and they use this skill to keep the conversation on point. But they do not pretend to know all the answers," a Harvard law professor told me several years ago. In that vein, I recently saw a very senior aerospace engineer appropriately cut off a young executive who had for weeks monopolized the weekly staff meeting with irrelevant tales of his own importance. "Stop!" the senior engineer finally said. "We do not need all that information. Think about the purpose of the meeting before you start telling twenty-five people everything you did last week." So, while it is essential to develop listening skills, you also need to develop the sense of when it is time to cut off the information flow or to redirect it. Do so with abrupt clarity.

Clear Channel

We have already discussed how confident executives surround themselves with bright, trustworthy people. Here is another essential quality for those with whom you surround yourself: clear, concise communication. The people I value most when I am gathering facts from a client to defend a lawsuit are those who: (1) can state their points in less than thirty seconds; and (2) can transcend the language or jargon of their specific professional discipline in a way that makes the point understandable by a smart but inexperienced layperson.

I have a couple of little indicators that tell me if I am working with people who will provide me clear channels of communication. You should develop your own, but try these out. First, ask yourself, How long are their voice mails? If someone leaves a rambling four-minute voice mail filled with "aahs," "ums," and repetitive statements, that person has a communication problem. I expect voice mails that are short, well-constructed, and make the point only one time.

Second, if someone uses trade jargon that you, as a layperson, obviously would not understand, that means that the person operates in a small world with blinders and is unable to facilitate the flow of information around and up the structure of an organization. For example, I once witnessed a civilian employee of the Department of Defense brief a diplomat of a foreign country on which U.S. military officials would attend a function that the diplomat was hosting. It was no secret that this particular diplomat had little or no military background. The Department of Defense employee told him approximately the following: "There will be two senior military officials present—CINCSOC and CINCPAC—they may have some SOCOM, USACOM, or CNO personnel with them, maybe a JAG or DOJ guy or gal will tag along. A couple of LAs from the INTEL committee always weasel their way in too." It was obvious that the diplomat had no idea who was coming to his social event, and it was amazing to me that the speaker was so caught up in his little world of acronyms that he could not see how ineffective his communication style was. The liaison was unable to recognize the differing perspective that the diplomat had, and could not, therefore, communicate effectively.

Multiple Channels

When you establish corporate or other organizational structures, you should focus "less on how a task is to be performed and more on how information will be developed and cross-checked," according to auto executive Jack Schmitt, whom we met earlier. You do this with a system of "corporate checks and balances," according to Marriott executive vice president Joe Ryan. "You've got to have some tension so that one arm of the entity does not completely take over the other one," adds Ryan.

To do so, you never let too much information reside in only one place. Ron Gafford of Austin Industries notes that "the people who tend to succeed in management are those who are good delegators and who have proper controls in place (checks and balances) to keep the ship upright. Those controls might include internal audit, contract reviews, separation of responsibilities, and controls that 'close the loop' on all open issues of importance to a company." He and others make use of independent assessment teams. Unless there is a serious legal or accounting issue involved, these independent teams do not have to be outside consultants. But you do use people from the organization who are not directly involved in the day-to-day operations of the group in question.

Finally, you establish staff meetings, off-site retreats, weekly teleconferences, and other methods that provide a forum for people to speak their minds. As we discussed briefly before, it is very easy for successful executives to isolate themselves and rely very heavily on one or two people whom they trust. Self-important executives also rely too heavily on the organizational chart, believing that they should only associate with people at an equal, greater, or slightly lower rank than themselves. These management methods are sure routes to the information blockage that can ultimately bring an organization or an individual down.

Wring the Emotion
out of Risk Analysis

📷 **SNAPSHOT**

Do you enjoy taking risks?

Yes: 30 percent   **No:** 70 percent

It is a new trend. Susan is the executive vice president of a publicly traded software company. Another company offers her the title of CEO. It looks like the chance of a lifetime. On a personal level, she is very excited. But she does not jump at the opportunity. Rather, she forces herself to remain cool to the idea of becoming a CEO. Instead, she hires a "due diligence" consultant—who has neither her emotional attachment to the idea of being a CEO nor the new company's incentive to paint a distortedly rosy picture of the job—to help her evaluate the risks associated with taking the new job. She wants a full assessment of (1) the financial status of the company, (2) its reputation for ethics, (3) the work environment and corporate politics, (4) the reason that the previous CEO left, and (5) the level of customer and shareholder satisfaction. And she wants it from an independent outsider, not someone who will put the best spin on the facts. Susan does not want to take the risk of walking into an Enron, Adelphia, Tyco, or Global Crossing in the making. Only after every stone is turned over and the company looks clean does she take the job.

One of the fatal flaws of near-invincible executives is that "they jump too quick," according to top prosecutor and attorney Ed Dowd. Truly invincible executives get no thrill out of taking risks, so they take the time to evaluate risks carefully and do not become so "invested" in their first favorable impression of a deal that they tune out the negatives that they later discover.

Reasonable Risk

Top professionals do not like risk, but they recognize that few people succeed in a big way without taking significant risks. A lot of professionals are "totally risk averse," according to Doug Bain of Boeing, "because they don't want to take responsibility for things going wrong. However, the higher you go up in the food chain, the less you see that, and the more people are willing to take reasonable risks." The key to successful risk taking is a skeptical, unemotional, and analytic approach to risk management. People who get "risk rushes"—as an executive of Westar Corporation once described it to me in a critical way—might enjoy a few victories, but they will tend to lose it all on one of their big gambles. For example, many senior executives of conglomerates that went around acquiring companies left and right during the 1990s got caught up in the "risk rush" mentality, and they are paying a dear price for that approach today.

A residential real estate agent who read my book on avoiding financial risk lamented to me, "It might sound strange, but I spend a lot of time trying to talk young couples *out* of buying a particular house. They fall in love with the first impression and they then become blinded to the plumbing and roofing problems and the fact that they really cannot afford the home. Yet so rarely can I convince them to go for something a little more reliable and a little more modest. Two years later the house is back on the market, and half the time there is a divorce to go along with it." Vulnerable executives often make exactly the same mistake. A business acquisition or transaction looks so appealing at first glance that they ignore, downplay, or distort the true risks when they become apparent. A few months or a couple of years down the road, disaster strikes.

Tom Gunn, who has sold more commercial and military aircraft than just about anyone in the world, notes that "the person who loves the least controls the relationship." That means if you become too wedded to the idea of a deal or transaction, the person on the other side is in total control, and you bear all the risk.

The disdain for risk that is common among top professionals causes them to evaluate the potential downside of every deal or opportunity in a detached, unemotional manner. In fact, they tend to take specific steps designed to wring the emotion out of their decision making—to objectify the process. There are three ways to obtain this objectification—and many senior managers use them all.

1. **Have outside help.** Hire a qualified, trustworthy outsider to investigate the risk for you, as Susan did in the example at the beginning of this chapter when she was considering the offer to become a CEO. While invincible executives tend to believe that companies overuse consultants in "soft" areas such as marketing, branding, and strategic planning, they almost all agree that organizations tend to underuse consultants as objective reviewers of specific risk points in potential projects or deals. "You have to put the appropriate team together to evaluate risk, and that includes outsiders, where necessary," according to Richard Bell, CEO of HDR,

Inc. The outside viewpoint ensures that your in-house staff has not become "collectively jaded," as one management consultant put it.

2. **Get it in writing.** The second way effective managers evaluate and reduce risk is through the development of a standardized, written risk evaluation process. Tom O'Neill, CEO of Parsons Brinckerhoff, a New York–based engineering firm with annual revenues of over $1 billion, recommends that, when projects with serious risk present themselves, the process of risk identification and analysis should be reduced to writing.

There are three parts to such a process: risk identification, factual development, and risk analysis. For example, when Parsons Brinckerhoff considers bidding on a construction project, the executives involved in the project must fill out a set of forms. Based upon prior experience of the company, the forms identify the major risks attendant to construction projects, such as the likelihood that the project will not proceed, currency fluctuation risks for foreign transactions, reliability of subcontractors, liquidated damages provisions for delays, uncertainties about the site of the construction, labor issues, issues with obtaining appropriate government approvals, etc.

Then qualified people gather facts about each risk and write them down. Based upon the facts, each potential risk is analyzed and a risk factor is assigned to the project based upon that analysis. "By the time it gets to me," O'Neill says, "the decision as to whether to proceed has practically been made." Through this process, biases, emotions, and instincts are supplanted with reason and analysis. As a result, the decision becomes easy.

3. **Develop ways to quantify the risk.** The third way effective managers wring the emotion out of decisions concerning risk is through *quantitative analysis*. A critical part of the quantitative risk

analysis process involves "developing clear reference points that will determine your rate of return on an investment," notes Richard Bell of HDR, Inc. You have to develop specific, reliable economic models that translate the risk into dollars and cents.

But quantitative risk analysis means much more than reliable profit projections. It means outperforming the competition. During his twenty-seven-year tenure as CEO of Anheuser-Busch, August Busch III increased the market share of his company from 25 percent to 49 percent, while the share of his nearest competitor dwindled to 19 percent. Many industry analysts attribute a lot of this success to Mr. Busch's decision to use computer models to assist in such areas as brewery location and targeted marketing. Mr. Busch began to use such methods in the 1970s, when most Americans had barely even heard of computers.

Sam Fox's company, Harbour Group, has turned around over one hundred floundering manufacturing companies over the past three decades, and he too attributes a lot of its success to the innovations in "statistical process control"—the development of reliable quantitative methodologies that measure the quality and reliability of manufacturing processes.

The Washington University Medical Center is consistently ranked as one of the top five medical treatment and training facilities in the United States in many areas of medicine. The center works hard to maintain its hard-earned reputation. Two of its top lawyers, Executive Vice-Chancellor and General Counsel Michael Cannon (a Rhodes Scholar and graduate of Yale Law School) and Deputy General Counsel Mark Eggert (a graduate of Harvard College and Law School), use a sophisticated software program to evaluate the legal risk associated with any claim that a doctor at the center performed in a substandard way. That program helps them determine whether there is liability, and if so, how great the liability is. "You cannot rely solely upon the numbers when you evaluate risk, but having the added dimension of a quantitative analysis helps keep the multiple variables and emotional aspects of any given risk situation in control," according to Eggert. They consider their quantitative tools as an essential element of a broader risk management and evaluation process.

Invincible executives stay on the leading edge of technology. Technology adds that essential element of detachment to any risky situation. Successful managers do not have to understand every aspect of the technology applicable to their fields, but they have to know enough to do two things: authorize value-added technological tools and reject the unnecessary bells and whistles that the tech geeks will try to sell them.

RULE
26

Take Decisive Action
to End Discord

▌●▐ SNAPSHOT

Do you personally intervene in personality conflicts among those with whom you work?

Yes: 84 percent **No:** 16 percent

We have discussed how management by intimidation interferes with information flow and creativity. We discussed in Rule 25 how emotion interferes with risk analysis. Indeed, it is a common thread in the interviews that I conducted that emotion interferes with organizational goals such as making money, producing quality products, or providing effective services. It follows, therefore, that invincible executives do not tolerate festering emotional conflicts among their employees.

Every time two people will not work well together, that conflict creates an inefficiency in the organization. That inefficiency costs money and hurts the product. Consequently, invincible executives learn to work with competent people whom they do not like, and they require others to do so as well. "I don't have to like you. I don't have to socialize with you after work. But we've got a corporate goal here and we better well do it," according to top Anheuser-Busch executive Stephen Lambright. Because conflict hurts the bottom line, very few top professionals adopt a hands-off approach to personality conflicts among employees. In fact, resolving conflict is "a significant part of the job" of managing people, according to top banker Drew Baur.

"I am the court of last resort," says Tom O'Neill of Parsons Brinckerhoff. "I give my people a chance to resolve a conflict by themselves, but if they can't, I do it for them," O'Neill notes. He considers himself to be the "anchor" for the company—the person who is always on an even keel himself and the person whose job it is to keep everyone else on an even keel as well. Resolving conflict is an essential part of being an effective CEO, according to O'Neill.

Doug Bain, the general counsel of Boeing, notes that keeping a group of motivated lawyers from fighting with one another is no easy task. Consequently, he is very direct about resolving such conflicts. His approach is "you and I do not have to like each other but we've got to work together." And what are the consequences of not working well together? "The consequence is you leave the company." This decisive approach to resolving conflict is common among executives who have staying power.

Two Approaches to Conflict Processes

The most successful professionals "accept talent in any package," says Joe Ryan of Marriott. They are tolerant of the personality differences among people and they require others to be so as well. When diverse personalities clash, good managers will step right in to fix the problem. They tend to use one of two processes for conflict resolution. A substantial minority of executives, including Janet Reno, deal with fighting employees by meeting with the employees individually or with their supervisors. A slight majority, however, including Hendrik Verfaillie, ex-CEO of Monsanto, Juanita Hinshaw of Graybar, and Doug Bain of Boeing, meet with the two feuding parties together.

The advantage of individual meetings is that you can be more severe in your comments about the conduct of the individual with whom you are speaking. "But meeting individually with people who are fighting at work can lead to paranoia and fear of favoritism," an Anheuser-Busch manager noted. Most, therefore, call both combatants into the office. The executive who is mediating the dispute will normally give the fighting parties a chance to air their concerns. A majority of senior executives will limit the time for airing concerns to five or ten minutes. Then, the senior executive will tell the fighters that their jobs depend upon the successful resolution of the problem and ask how they propose to resolve it. As ideas come forward, the senior executive pushes on each person to give a little bit on his or her position until they have arrived at a compromise. You may even consider having the combatants write down the compromise and sign it.

Do Not Mediate a Transgression

The two approaches outlined above work 95 percent of the time. But there is an assumption built into both of these processes: no one is really *right or wrong*. When an executive has to deal with a personality conflict, each person involved in the conflict is convinced that he or she has been terribly wronged by the other. But 95 percent of the time, when the neutral senior executive looks at the issue with a more objective set of eyes, what he or she finds is a personality conflict with no clear right or wrong.

Every now and then, however, the personality conflict is the result of one person having committed a clear wrong and the other person being clearly in the right. In such situations, you, as the arbiter of the dispute, must throw compromise out the door. You cannot, for example, compromise when one employee is committing sexual harassment against another. You cannot compromise when one employee is advocating a legally questionable accounting tactic or a course of action that would breach the organization's contracts or regulatory requirements. Many top executives have been ruined by scandal when they tried to mediate a situation where there was clear wrongdoing. The result is that the executive is eventually accused of tolerating and tacitly condoning improper or unethical conduct—and the accusation often comes by way of a civil rights or whistleblower lawsuit, or, in the worst cases, a federal investigation. It only happens about 5 percent of the time, but you have to be on the lookout for situations where "personality conflicts" are the result of clearly unethical or improper behavior on the part of an employee. In such cases there is no room for compromise. You discipline or fire the offending party and you commend the person who reported it.

Outside Disputes

Bill Stowers is a senior Boeing executive who manages relationships with hundreds of Boeing's subcontractors. With that many suppliers to manage, there are always a few disputes going on at any given time. Stowers is a big fan of "senior official presentations" to resolve these disputes—you bring in high-level officials who are not otherwise involved in the dispute. He has established this method because it eliminates the emotional element of a dispute, as well as the attendant filtering of information that comes when people become emotionally involved in a business problem.

Here is why and how it works. Often disputes with customers and suppliers can be traced to personality conflicts between your employees and theirs. The customer might be claiming that you are mismanaging his or her company's account when, in fact, the customer just does not get along with your program manager. When your organization has a dispute with a customer or supplier, never let the emotions get out of hand. It is important that you and your counterpart in the other organization get together as early as possible to attempt to resolve the dispute. One method that has shown to be effective is to invite a high-level counterpart on the other side who has no direct personal involvement in the dispute. That person brings in his or her staff members that are involved in the dispute and they give an uninterrupted presentation to you of their view on the issue. Then your people get to give a similar uninterrupted presentation to the other company's senior official. Usually the presentations are limited to one hour and include graphics and other visual presentation materials.

Then the senior officials get together to resolve the matter. Because the senior officials have no direct personal involvement in the dispute, they can eye the problem more objectively than the direct participants can. Again, by wringing out the emotional and personality issues, solutions to problems become much clearer. Stowers has resolved or avoided five major lawsuits through this method. "It has proven to be an extremely effective method of resolving disputes in an emotionally charged environment," he notes. And it has saved his company millions of dollars in legal fees as well.

27

Get Results Through Alignment and Adjustment, Not Democracy

📷 **SNAPSHOT**

Do you believe in corporate democracy?

Yes: 15 percent **No:** 85 percent

We have already established that executives who manage like dictators will rarely get to the top, and if they do, they probably will not stay there. "A good manager operates like a constitutional monarch," according to Ed Dowd. He or she retains the authority to override any other individual, but is still limited in his or her conduct by the rules and policies of the company and the legal restrictions applicable to the company.

"No one has absolute authority. The people who think they do start to mix personal and business activity, and before you know it they are under federal investigation," Dowd says. If you walk into an organization, ignore the culture and the rules, and simply say, "I am the new sheriff in town; they obviously brought me in because you guys were all screwed up and I'm going to show you how it's really done," your career will "crash and burn," according to Doug Bain of Boeing.

Indeed, if you get too swept up in your own authority, you will start to put your own interests above those of the organization. One only has to look at the CEO of Tyco International, who was indicted for allegedly channeling his personal art purchases through his company to avoid paying sales taxes. As soon as you feel you have total power, you will start to make these kinds of mistakes, and they will cost you everything.

Former Senator Bob Dole finds that the biggest flaw that causes the downfall of otherwise successful politicians is the "false sense of invincibility that comes with power." That often leads people to push the envelope on the belief that they can get away with anything—that no rules apply to their conduct or authority. Once you feel that you answer to no one, you are on the brink of professional disaster.

No Democracy

Does that mean that the invincible executive executes a more democratic management style? Not on your life. While delusions of absolute power have proven fatal to many corporate careers over the past couple of years, very few executives with whom I spoke embraced anything close to democracy in managing an organization. Mike Sears of Boeing puts it this way: "Somebody has to decide where we are going. And that is not something that we get to vote on. The leader has to decide. Then the leader has to get alignment."

The key word is *alignment*. It is a management approach that is somewhere in between dictatorship and democracy. According to Sears, "This alignment process is extremely important and very dependent on the ability of the leader to lead people—to get them to understand, to get them to agree, to get them to say that 'this is the right thing to do,' and to motivate them to get there as fast as they possibly can." Or, as Sears's coworker Doug Bain put it, you have to constantly "assess and obtain the buy-in" of your employees with respect to any decision that you make. The ability to obtain "buy-in" or alignment is an essential management skill in today's corporate world.

There are three steps to achieving effective alignment. Step one is the most democratic: get input. Sears and several of his counterparts in the corporate world emphasize the importance of getting a lot of input from a lot of people before the company makes a significant decision—such as launching a new product line or closing down an old one. "Listen as well as you communicate," notes Bill Shaw, president of Marriott International. Those who might be affected by the decision should feel that they had a chance to make their views known and that the ultimate decision factored in their concerns. " 'What do you think?' is the most important line in business," according to legendary CEO Bill Marriott.

Step two: the leader makes the decision. That is the simple step. There is no democracy there. The leader "lays out the vision" and, concurrently, provides an "action plan with priorities," so that no one can have doubts about what the decision is and how the company is going to get there, according to Bill Shaw.

Step three is motivating people to get with the program—whether they agree with the ultimate decision or not. That requires them to accept change—which is a very difficult process. The way top executives get people motivated to achieve the desired change and result quickly is through "communication and trust," according to Sears. "You have to inform, you have to repeat, you have to be open, you have to put the cards on the table, and you have to be willing to withstand somebody looking at you and questioning your decision." Sears also notes, "The more trust you have built up with people, the less they will question you." Bill Shaw of Marriott agrees with this aspect of the alignment process. "You have to communicate [the plan] simply, get people to buy into it, and then surround yourself with the good people who will execute."

In sum, Sears says, "The alignment process all comes down to whether you understand what we are trying to do. And you cannot just say 'yes.' That is unacceptable. I have to have this interaction with you so that I can be sure that you really do understand what I mean."

The Consistency Factor

Lieutenant General John Sams confirms that there is no place for democracy in a military organization, but he notes that it is essential that the leader apply a consistent set of principles. "As a commander, you want to be the most predictable person in the squadron," he notes. "You do not want people to wonder how you are going to react in a given situation. You want them to know. That is how you earn respect." Bill Shaw of Marriott agrees: "You need to be behaviorally predictable, because it is very hard for people to get behind someone who isn't."

Interestingly, General Sams believes that the loss of respect due to arbitrary action is often the result of wanting to be *liked too much*. We often think of arbitrary action as the hallmark of a ruthless tyrant. Not true, according to General Sams. He has seen many would-be leaders lose the respect of their subordinates because they tried too hard to be liked. General Sams tells young officers that within three days of being given command of a squadron, a junior officer or sergeant will walk into your office with a young airman in tow and tell you that this airman failed to meet some element of values the U.S. Air Force holds dear. For example, it could be as simple as a failure to meet weight standards. The sergeant will ask that you exercise your discretion not to ground or reprimand the young airman. After all, the airman is a good troop! You want the new squadron members to like you, and you will be very tempted to let the transgression go, or give him a second chance. As soon as you do it, however, you have taken the first step toward losing the respect of your squadron. Why? "Because when this guy walks out of your office and you did not take the action required by the regulations, every other overweight person in the squadron is going to know that you did not take the required action. And so when the next guy walks in overweight and you decide to take action, he is going to ask why you took action against him. At that point, your credibility is shot. And if the second individual is a minority, are you now treating him differently because of that? You cannot now take any action because any action looks like discrimination." You have given up your moral authority to command.

"You should not make it your goal to be liked by everyone. It is much more important to be predictable and consistent. That earns respect, which is much more important than being liked," according to General Sams.

Invincible executives are not tyrants; they do not feel that they make the rules or that they can transcend them. By the same token, they are not democrats. They call the shots, and they do not worry about being liked. Rather they earn the respect of those who work for them by (1) getting input from many people before making significant decisions; (2) making clear, unambiguous decisions; (3) communicating the decisions in a manner that motivates people to achieve the desired results quickly; and (4) building trust and confidence through the predictable and consistent application of the rules that he or she lays down as the organization works toward the desired results.

RULE

28

Minimize Meetings

📷 **SNAPSHOT**

Do you maintain strict control over meetings?

Yes: 85 percent   **No:** 15 percent

"Minimize meetings," says Bill Shaw, president of Marriott. Echoing the view of most corporate leaders, Bill Winter, chairman emeritus of Dr. Pepper/Seven Up, Inc., was quick to point out that too many organizations are "ahead of quota on meetings and under quota in sales." The conclusion is almost unanimous: invincible executives do not like meetings.

Another message from the top: when you do have meetings, keep them short. "I have never been to a meeting that really needed to last longer than a half hour," according to Tom O'Neill of Parsons Brinckerhoff. Some executives—like banker Drew Baur—add another half hour to Mr. O'Neill's time threshold: "My rule is no more than an hour. If it lasts more than an hour, I do not want to be part of it." Have no doubt, therefore, that the overwhelming majority of invincible executives do not like meetings and, consequently, maintain very strict control over meetings. They control (1) the time of the meeting, (2) the content of the meeting, and (3) the way that the meeting is recorded.

Start on Time; Flow Smoothly; Finish on Time

Over half of the invincible executives with whom I discussed the issue said that they always start a meeting on time. "It is unfair to the other people attending if you force them to wait for the stragglers," according to O'Neill. Doug Bain of Boeing echoes a similar sentiment: starting on time shows respect for those who arrived on time. Starting on time also lets people know that you value strict adherence to schedules, which is an important quality in any business context, and it tells people that you expect precision in their conduct. President Bush, for example, is so insistent that meetings start on time that almost everyone else invited arrives early to his meetings—sometimes a half hour early. Lieutenant General John Sams noted that the people who tended to do best in the air force were those who showed up early for their flight briefings.

When meetings start on time, the whole organization seems better run, more efficient, and more synergistic. Moreover, once stragglers feel the embarrassment of walking in late to a meeting in progress even one time, they will not be late again. That further increases the efficiency of the organization.

Next, you cannot interrupt the time-flow of a meeting. That means that cell phones and pagers should be off, and you should tell your secretary, assistant, or coworkers not to interrupt you during the meeting. When the ringing of a cell phone interrupts a meeting, the owner of that phone is effectively saying that he or she has something to do that is so much more important than the meeting that it is worth interrupting everyone at the meeting so that he or she can attend to the higher priority. That is arrogant, selfish—and a career killer. Once again, President Bush is the model—he detests cell phones going off in the middle of a meeting and gives people the "evil eye" when it happens. He also never forgets it, I am told. You need to keep your phone off and you need to insist that those working for you keep theirs off as well.

Finally, many top executives set time limits on meetings. They will open meetings with a line like, "I have an appointment outside the office in one hour, so this meeting has to be over in forty-five minutes." It is amazing how much self-aggrandizing baloney you can avoid in a meeting if everyone knows it has to end soon. The meeting naturally develops a fast, constructive pace that allows the business at hand to be completed, but culls out all the digressions and self-important comments that tend to dominate more meandering meetings. In fact, Bill Shaw of Marriott even allocates a specific amount of time to individual subjects that a meeting is supposed to cover.

Lead and Control

We discussed earlier the importance of taking any chance you can to lead. Meetings represent that chance. You should always volunteer to lead a meeting. Once you do so, however, you must take specific measures to control the content of the meeting. Virtually all of the top professionals I interviewed for this book—from top aerospace executive Tom Gunn to Marriott's Bill Shaw—use written agendas. Many provide that agenda before the meeting and a sizeable percentage put names next to each topic to tell the attendees who is expected to speak on which topic. That focuses the meetings and reduces digressions. Each person is so concerned about his or her designated topic that he or she is less likely to opine meaninglessly on some irrelevant subject.

In addition, while common courtesy is essential in a meeting, you cannot hesitate to cut off someone who is droning on too long or who is addressing a subject that will not advance the purpose of the meeting, according to Hendrik Verfaillie, former CEO of Monsanto. A sizeable percentage of senior executives reserve five minutes or so at the end of the meeting for "other issues." That five minutes gives the leader of the meeting a chance to defer marginally relevant topics to the end of the meeting.

Control the Record

The purpose of a meeting is to resolve a controversy or issue. During the course of this iterative process, a lot of people will present views that are ultimately rejected or substantially refined. Unfortunately, someone usually records in notes or minutes every little thing that anyone says. These notes or minutes frequently come back to haunt the organization should a dispute arise down the road.

Invincible executives tend to have someone they trust take the minutes—they never rely upon the other side in a negotiation or a dispute because the people on the other side will skew the minutes to reflect their viewpoints. Moreover, even with internal meetings, truly sharp executives will not let their people write "stream of consciousness" meeting minutes that document every disagreement or ridiculous idea that someone had. Rather, they insist that minutes identify the participants and the issues discussed and then record the resolution or consensus, according to Hendrik Verfaillie.

Top professionals despise an inefficiently run meeting. If you want to join their ranks, you have to arrive on time, turn off the cell phone, keep it short, stick to the subject, and record the results only. Then, as you rise up the corporate or organizational ladder, you must insist that those who work for you do exactly the same thing.

RULE

29

Negotiate the Opening and Closing Ceremonies, but Leave the Games to Others

📷 **SNAPSHOT**

Are you a good negotiator?

Yes: 40 percent   **No:** 60 percent

When I wrote the question, "Are you a good negotiator?" I expected to hear one invincible executive after the other tell me war stories of negotiations in which they had gotten everything they wanted and bled the other side dry. I expected confidence—even cockiness. I got a little of that, but not very much. The majority of top professionals with whom I discussed the issue of negotiations said that they did not like negotiating, and a majority of those said that they did not think they were very good at it. "I am never as good a negotiator as I want to be," says Dave Ruf—the entrenched, tough, and well-liked CEO of Burns & McDonnell. "When I get done, I always wonder how much I left on the table," he added. In fact, Mr. Ruf joked that "if *both sides* don't like it, it is probably the right deal." Not the kind of statements that you would expect of this self-confident ex-musician who toured the country and performed on the "Today" show when he was fourteen years old.

Ruf's counterpart at Parsons Brinckerhoff, Tom O'Neill, candidly stated, "Actually, I don't think I am good at negotiating. I am too honest and I like to get to the point. Negotiations drag on." Other top executives said virtually the same thing. Even the respected and successful Senator John Danforth, who sometimes represents companies in ethical dilemmas, lamented that the government "always seems to get the better of me when I am trying to work out a deal." His clients do not feel that way—they love him and the results he gets. But, like so many other accomplished executives, *he feels that way*.

Is it true that top executives not only dislike negotiating but also are bad at it? Certainly, they do not like it. Top executives express their disdain for negotiating with conviction and sincerity. However, after talking to colleagues of these leaders, I have concluded with a high degree of confidence that invincible executives are much better at negotiating than they might admit or even believe. Most of them have had great success in building their organizations since they have been in positions of power, and you do not expand a business or similar organization without negotiating favorable relationships with customers, suppliers, joint venturers, and takeover targets. So, assuming, therefore, that leading professionals are better negotiators than they let on, why don't they like negotiating deals?

I Can't Dance

First, invincible executives hate bull. Negotiations are full of it. Tom O'Neill says he cannot stand the "dance" of a negotiation. Specific elements of the dance include: (1) when you pretend to need one price and say it is your final offer, but you know that you will come down if you have to; (2) when you walk out and say you are never coming back only to be back the next day; or (3) when the time comes where everyone sees where the compromise process is leading but you can't just say, "OK, we all know this is the right number" or your right number becomes a new number for the other side to negotiate downward. "I just find the whole process distasteful," O'Neill says—echoing many others.

As a result, a large number of top executives avoid whenever possible direct involvement in negotiating specific deals such as a customer relationship, a merger, or an employment agreement with a subordinate. Make no mistake—they have people report progress on a near real-time basis. They provide extensive input. They just avoid direct participation—with two exceptions. They limit their direct involvement to the front end or the back end of a negotiation—"the opening and closing ceremonies," as a construction executive once told me. For example, one CEO may get together with the CEO of another company and "agree in principle"—a one-page agreement—that they will *pursue* an exclusive joint venture, but then they leave it up to the contracts, financial, and legal people to negotiate the deal. Like many others of his caliber, Tom Gunn, the former top marketing and sales executive at McDonnell Douglas (and a licensed attorney), told me that he very much enjoys structuring the general framework and essential terms of a deal, but then he steps aside and lets others handle the specifics.

According to Jack Walbran, a long-time Boeing lawyer who has worked with many a CEO, top executives also do not mind coming in at the end to close the deal with a "sweetener"—one last concession out of the blue, often a deal-enhancing product, service, or financial arrangement unrelated to the current negotiations, that the organization has held in its hip pocket until the end of the negotiations process.

This is a process similar to the senior official presentations that I advocated when discussing dispute resolution earlier in the book. For example, I recently witnessed two companies try to settle a major lawsuit. One company agreed to pay the other $2 million, but the other wanted $3 million and the parties were at an impasse. The company that had offered $2 million had its CEO call the CEO of the other company and offer a guarantee that another division of his company would give at least $1 million in subcontracts to the other company over the next five years if the other company would accept the $2 million cash offer. That closed the deal immediately. Top people put themselves in a position where they are the opener—the person who initiates an idea for a venture—or the closer—the person who puts the final touches on the deal and gets the handshake. They leave the grinding to others where possible.

Going back to the dance metaphor, executives who enjoy long-term success say that they put themselves in a position where they can initiate the dance or finish it, but they avoid the hours, days, or weeks, of tangoing in between.

When You *Do* Have to Do the Grunt Work

Of course, while you should try to get there, you may not be in a position in your organization to avoid being on the front lines of negotiations. Most of us are required to slog in the negotiation mud on many occasions as we work our way up the professional ladder. But even so, there are a couple of strategies you can adopt to enhance your status in your organization as you participate in negotiations, and they relate directly to what we have discussed in the preceding paragraphs.

First, come up with suggestions for new business relationships for your organization. Be the one who assists the CEO or other top executive in formulating the "agreement in principle" that gets the negotiations started. If you are in on the front end of a deal, you will get some extra credit when the deal finally closes. Second, think of possible "sweeteners" and propose them to the boss as a way to get the deal done. Then watch happily as the boss gets the credit for closing the deal with a sweetener you have developed. The boss will never forget that you made him or her look good. You will get the next promotion—it works like a charm. As counsel to several large companies, I have seen just that situation happen literally dozens of times.

Tactical Versus Strategic Thinking

Another reason top executives do not like negotiations is that negotiations are very tactical—i.e., focused on specific, often short-term, gains and concessions. People who make it to the top usually have good tactical skills, but they do not like using them. They prefer looking at long-term relationships and the long-term health of their organizations. "I want a deal that is fair, not necessarily the most lucrative one we could squeeze out of the customer," says Ruf of Burns & McDonnell. The reason that he and others feel that way is simple. "Eighty percent of our business is repeat business," says Richard Bell of HDR, Inc. "I cannot let short-term gain ruin long-term prospects. That is why I advocate fairness over being greedy in a negotiation." Dave Ruf pointed out that his company's first client from 102 years ago remains a client today, and you do not develop that kind of relationship by squeezing every nickel out of the client during a negotiation.

This overriding concern for long-term relationships tends to make top executives a little "softer" when they were negotiating—occasionally too soft if you listen to the subordinates of some of the people I interviewed. "Once our CEO is convinced we will make a fair profit if we do our job well, he loses interest in squeezing another nickel out of the other side," a senior engineer at a software development company lamented to me after a long negotiation with a client of mine a few years back.

Because people who make it to the top think constructively and long-term, the whole process of negotiations—which involves breaking the other side down and getting specific terms right now—is distasteful to them. Negotiations are emotional, and top executives stay out of emotional situations. Negotiations involve gamesmanship, and top executives hate ploys. If you want to be the invincible executive, therefore, you need to develop your "front end" and "back end" skills early in your career by putting yourself in a position to advise your top management on the initial structuring and the ultimate closing of deals. That is where the real action is. Then bite your lip and participate in the "dance" as necessary—always making it your goal to extricate yourself from that process as soon as possible in your career. And the best way to advance from the negotiation dance is to *make the boss look good*.

30

Put the Interests of the Organization Over the Interests of Individuals—Very Carefully

📷 **SNAPSHOT**

When you make decisions, do you put the organization or individuals first?

Organization: 82 percent   **Individuals:** 18 percent

Most professionals with staying power learn to put organizational interests above the interests of individual employees or other people who might be adversely affected by business decisions. But making the organization paramount is a very tricky process. Obviously, by putting the organization first, top professionals believe that they are looking out for the greater good of their employees, shareholders, and business partners. But they recognize that these organizational decisions can literally devastate individual lives. If you want to get to the top, therefore, you have to be willing to take action that will hurt people whom you like if the interests of the organization so require. But there are some important rules that you must follow if you are to pull this strategy off successfully.

Mike Sears of Boeing tries to develop close professional bonds with the executives working for him. Yet he stated to me in no uncertain terms that if a friend is not performing well, he will without hesitation remove that friend from his or her position. It is tough, but it has to be done—the organization comes first. His former boss, Harry Stonecipher, had to downsize St. Louis operations substantially after the merger of McDonnell-Douglas and Boeing—reducing the St. Louis operation from forty thousand to less than seventeen thousand employees. The long-term viability of the organization required this downsizing. Thousands of people were hurt, but Stonecipher did not hesitate to do what the organization required.

American presidents have for over two centuries made decisions that adversely affected the lives of thousands of Americans when the interests of our democracy required such a policy. Most recently, after September 11, 2001, President Bush, supported by Vice President Cheney, issued an order that the U.S. military was to shoot down any hijacked commercial jetliner that was heading toward a city. That directive means our own forces will likely kill two hundred or more Americans should another terrorist hijacking occur. Why? For the greater good. The president decided that sacrificing two hundred lives was better than the uncertainty of how many lives might be lost if the plane were crashed into a building, and that it was even worth sacrificing those lives for the possibility that a major symbol of our country—the Washington Monument, the Statue of Liberty, etc.—would be destroyed. He made the tough decision that the risk of greater casualties or the psychological devastation of seeing a major monument in flames was worth two hundred innocent lives. This was a tough but necessary decision in the minds of most Americans.

There can be no doubt, therefore, that organizational interests must prevail if you are to become an executive with staying power. However, putting organizational interests above individual interests is a process that is fraught with risk. Invincible executives manage to put the organization first without engendering career-fatal levels of resentment against them.

In order to be able to put the organization first successfully, you have to follow some pretty strict rules or your career will come tumbling down. Let's go over them.

You Can't Hurt Others While Enriching Yourself

"All you really have in this world is your credibility," says former Senator Bob Dole. That point has been vividly illustrated in the corporate world over the last couple of years. CEOs who have paid themselves tens of millions of dollars while laying off thousands of workers have lost all credibility in the business community. They got away with it in the booming 1990s, but they will not get away with it anymore. If your company or organization is performing badly enough that you need to cut staff, benefits, or salaries, *you have to share in the pain.* Even if you are at midlevel, one manager at an automaker said, "You need to suffer with everyone else." This gentleman decided to forgo a raise the year he had to lay off seven people in his department. It was not that painful for him, but it was a priceless gesture on his part.

The ImClone insider trading scandal that ensnared Martha Stewart was big news because it looked like an elite group was abusing its position of power while everyday people suffered the losses. The numerous instances that have surfaced where companies lent their executives millions of dollars out of the corporate treasury greatly added to the career woes of those who got the loans once the companies experienced problems. The secret partnerships that enriched individual Enron executives proved fatal to the careers of the executives who thought that they could profit at the expense of shareholders and employees.

Executives and their careers can survive economic or business downturns. They cannot survive such downturns when the downturns are coupled with evidence that they got sweetheart deals, quietly and secretly enriching themselves prior to or even during the downturn. The scrutiny and criticism will be unbearable in such situations.

Individual Symbols

While the organization comes first, invincible executives recognize the importance of putting a human face on the organization. Consequently, they frequently use individual employees as symbols of the good of the entity. Each year, for example, in their State of the Union Addresses, both President Clinton and President Bush have made a point of bringing ordinary Americans who have done something extraordinary to the halls of Congress to give them recognition in front of the whole U.S. government and all of the American citizens watching.

Successful corporate executives and military officers also make it a regular practice to single out people—at every level of the organization—who have performed exceptionally. They do not devalue the process by giving awards to everyone, nor do they devalue the process by just signing some certificate or sending a medal through interoffice mail. Rather, they make sure that they learn of true accomplishment in their organization, and they participate directly in the process of rewarding that accomplishment.

"Ceremonies—albeit brief ones—are a must," according to top prosecutor Ed Dowd. It makes the individual receiving recognition proud, but more important, it tells everyone that the organization is paramount. The ceremony reminds people of the reverence that the top executives have for their organization. You want your people framing their awards and putting them on the walls.

Know the Limits of Organizational Priority

Organizational priority has its limits, however. In the 1970s, a jury found Ford Motor Company liable for hundreds of millions of dollars because it had decided not to make improvements on the Pinto automobile—improvements that allegedly could have saved hundreds of lives. Ford had allegedly performed a cost-benefit analysis and determined that the company would do better financially paying off the families of those who were killed than it would if it simply fixed the problem. The country was outraged at the decision to put profits above lives. In not less than twenty publicized cases since then, companies were found to have performed cost-benefit analyses where they put a value on human life and made a decision to allow an unsafe product to stay on the market. In each case, the careers of those who made these decisions ended—some with jail time.

You could argue that these executives were looking out for the greater financial good of their companies when they made these unfortunate decisions. *There are, however, outer limits to the concept of greater good.* The principal limits are the health and safety of others—the safety of your customers and the safety of your employees. Top executives never scrimp, cut corners, or compromise safety. Cost-benefit analyses go out the window when human health is weighing in on one side of the scale.

This rule applies at all levels of organizational decision making—from taking whatever steps are necessary to remedy a product defect, to ensuring that female employees who work late do not have to walk to a parking garage alone, to monitoring the air quality in the work spaces of employees who work in warehouses. The thumb goes down on the scale heavily in favor of safety-related costs and decisions.

Communication and Compassion

Finally, if you are going to make a decision that will hurt people in your organization, you have to couple that decision with an explanation that is honest, direct, and compassionate. You do not just announce a layoff in a three-line memo, for example. You explain in a succinct and heartfelt manner the reason why the layoff is necessary. You give people time to leave or retire on their own, if possible. You discuss why alternatives are not viable. You must also provide some support in terms of serious career placement services, a respectful severance arrangement, and other evidence that you want to mitigate the adverse effects the organizational decision will have on individual lives. "You should always spend more money than you legally or contractually have to on these types of mitigating services," according to a human resources director at a major law firm. "It helps those who are displaced by the decision and it boosts the morale of those who are staying."

Conclusion

It is perhaps the most delicate task of the executive with staying power: to remain focused on the good of the organization while showing compassion and concern for the interests of the individuals who make up the organization. The skill will, however, come almost naturally if you follow the other Rules of Invincibility discussed in the preceding sections. Maintaining the interests of the organization without destroying the morale of its components requires a leader who shows the kind of flexibility that we discussed in Part I, the even-tempered demeanor that we discussed in Part II, and the ability to obtain a reliable flow of information that we discussed in Part III.

Once you start implementing the strategies of the invincible executives we have discussed in this book, the ability to advance your organization without losing the respect of the individuals who make up that organization will come almost naturally. As you refine that skill, your legend will grow around you without any specific action or effort on your part to enhance your status. When you start to notice that natural momentum developing in your career, you have advanced far down the road to ensuring long-term professional success. Before you know it, I'll be knocking on your door for an interview. You will be the newest invincible executive. You will have staying power.

Appendix

List of Those Profiled

The following executives were profiled for this book. A single asterisk indicates an executive with whom I conducted a formal interview. Three interviewees preferred to remain anonymous, as referenced in the text. In some instances, I made minor alterations to their stories (dates, locations, product lines, and so forth) to protect the identities of those who might be embarrassed.

*Douglas G. Bain
Senior Vice President and General Counsel,
The Boeing Company

*Andrew N. "Drew" Baur
Chairman and CEO, Southwest Bank

*Richard R. Bell
Chairman, CEO, and President, HDR, Inc.

William O. Boykin
Major General, United States Special Operations Command

Charles Brennan
Radio Announcer

Michael Cannon
Executive Vice-Chancellor and General Counsel,
Washington University

*****Norma B. Clayton**
Vice President–General Manager, Aerospace Support Center—
Maintenance and Modification, The Boeing Company

William Jefferson "Bill" Clinton
Former President of the United States

*****Adam Clymer**
Washington Correspondent, the *New York Times*

William Cohen
Former United States Senator and Secretary of Defense

Adam Creighton
Former Center, Chicago Blackhawks and other NHL teams

*****Sheryl Crow**
Singer, Songwriter

*****John C. "Jack" Danforth**
United States Senator (retired);
Special Counsel, Waco Investigation;
Special Envoy to the Sudan; Partner, Bryan Cave LLP

James DeVita
Former Assistant United States Attorney

*Robert J. "Bob" Dole
Former United States Senator

*Edward L. "Ed" Dowd Jr.
Former United States Attorney, numerous Department of
Justice posts

Joseph Durant
CEO, Westar Corp.

Mark Eggert
Deputy General Counsel, Washington University

*Patrick J. "Pat" Finneran Jr.
Vice President and General Manager,
Navy and Marine Corps Programs, The Boeing Company

*Samuel "Sam" Fox
Chairman and CEO (Founder), The Harbour Group, Ltd.

*Ronald J. Gafford
President and CEO, Austin Industries

*Richard A. Gephardt
Congressman, Former Minority Leader, United States House
of Representatives

*Joel Gotler
Joel Gotler & Associates

*Earl G. Graves
Chairman and CEO, Founder, and Publisher,
Black Enterprise magazine

*Thomas M. "Tom" Gunn
Senior Vice President of Business Development (retired),
McDonnell Douglas Corporation

Dr. William Hamree
Former Deputy Secretary of Defense

Ronald Henderson
United States Marshall and former Police Chief, St. Louis

*Juanita H. Hinshaw
Senior Vice President and CFO,
Graybar Electric Company, Inc.

Eric Holder
Former Deputy Attorney General

Walter Jockety
General Manager, St. Louis Cardinals

Virginia Johnson
Sexual Researcher and Author (deceased)

Roger Kennedy
Former Director of the Smithsonian Institution

*Dr. Joshua Korzenik
Assistant Professor, Washington University School of Medicine

*Stephen K. Lambright
Group Vice President and General Counsel,
Anheuser-Busch Companies, Inc.

William Lindsley
Former Franchise Owner, *The Princeton Review*

*Christopher "Chris" Lloyd
Television Executive Producer, "Frasier," and other television shows

*J. W. "Bill" Marriott Jr.
Chairman and CEO, Marriott International, Inc.

William Masters
Sexual Researcher and Author (deceased)

Walter L. Metcalfe Jr.
Chairman, Bryan Cave LLP

Patrick G. Murphy
United States District Judge

Sandra Day O'Connor
Associate Justice, United States Supreme Court

*Thomas J. "Tom" O'Neill
President and CEO, Parsons Brinckerhoff, Inc.

James C. Palmer
Director, The Beekman Estate

*James F. "Jim" Parker
CEO and Vice Chairman of the Board, Southwest Airlines

Richard Parker
Professor of Law, Harvard Law School

Aaron Priest
Literary Agent

*Admiral Joseph Prueher
Commander in Chief of the Pacific Fleet;
United States Ambassador to the People's Republic of China
(retired)

William H. Rehnquist
Chief Justice, United States Supreme Court

*Janet Reno
Former Attorney General of the United States

*Dave G. Ruf Jr.
Chairman and CEO, Burns & McDonnell

*Joseph Ryan
Executive Vice President and General Counsel, Marriott
International, Inc.

*Lt. Gen. John B. Sams Jr.
Commander, Fifteenth Air Force (retired)

*Jack Schmitt
Owner, CEO, The Jack Schmitt Companies

*Bruno Schmitter
President and CEO, Hydromat, Inc./Turmatic Systems, Inc.

Peter Schoomaker
General, United States Special Operations Command (retired)

*****Michael M. "Mike" Sears**
Executive Vice President and CFO, The Boeing Company

Charles Shaw
United States District Judge

*****William "Bill" Shaw**
President and COO, Marriott International, Inc.

Wendy Sherman
Literary Agent

*****Gina Shock**
Drummer, the Go-Go's

*****Alan K. Simpson**
Former United States Senator

Arlen Specter
United States Senator

William L. Stowers
Vice President, Supplier Management and Procurement,
The Boeing Company

*****Barrett A. Toan**
Chairman and CEO, Express Scripts, Inc.

Clyde C. Tuggle
Vice President and Director of Worldwide Communications, Coca-Cola

*Hendrik A. Verfaillie
Former President and CEO, Monsanto Company

Joseph D. Whitley
Partner, Alston & Bird, former Associate Attorney General

*William "Bill" Winter
Chairman Emeritus, Dr. Pepper/Seven Up, Inc.

Index